Anyone can do a PhD

Successful Strategies to Complete a PhD Program

Dr. Raghu Korrapati
Ph.D., D.Sc., D.Litt.

AF657960

DIAMOND BOOKS
www.diamondbook.in

Publisher	:	**Diamond Pocket Books (P) Ltd.** X-30, Okhla Industrial Area, Phase-II New Delhi-110020
Phone	:	011- 40712200
E-mail	:	sales@dpb.in
Website	:	www.diamondbook.in
Edition	:	2022
Printed by	:	Adarsh Printers, Delhi- 110032

Anyone can do a PhD

Author – Dr. Raghu Korrapati

To

MNR

Preface

Understanding why Students Don't Complete Ph.D Program, Mitigate Risks, and Have a Practical Strategy to Successful Completion

Anyone can do a Doctor of Philosophy (PhD), not necessarily a brilliant person but someone who is basically ready to put in the much-needed effort, persist, and manage his/her time well. Practically, it entails making up one's mind to give up a significant chunk of one's life for a particular period of time in order to accomplish something where the reward is mostly personal. PhD completion can be accomplished if one is motivated by personal reward rather than by the values of one's social group. Research shows that while students with varying mindset have the potential to complete PhD across all groups, those with clearly stated personal goals appear to make the best progress. Most people regard PhD as a mystical goal that can only be achieved by a special group of people, but it is actually a social and academic construct that can only be achieved with the proper intelligence, determination, commitment, persistence, and resilience.

The goal of this book is quite simply to understand the potential reasons for dropping out of a Ph.D. program and offer strategies to successfully complete this prestigious program. Despite their best efforts and ambitions, many are unable to endure till the end of this comprehensive and demanding program. In the chapters to follow, we will uncover some of the major causes for this problem, such as individual characteristics, supervisor and student relationship, time management, lack of candidate's ability, student engagement, financial incapability, quality of interaction and mentoring. To better understand the problem, the book also highlights the results of a comparative study of Ph.D. dropout rates with those of community college, bachelors, and masters program. Using data from three studies on student attrition, this book also takes a closer look at the research methods regularly used to study attrition data. Descriptive statistics, univariate, hierarchical and multiple logistic regression analyses were found to be regularly used. The book concludes with recommendations and future research direction to forestall futuristic dropout of doctoral students.

Contents

Chapter 1
Why Doctoral Students Dropout of PhD Program

1. Introduction

Doctor of Philosophy (PhD) attainment is known to be a prestigious and challenging venture that plays an essential role in creating new knowledge and developing new skills, thereby needing a high level of commitment. However, high attrition rates, delay, and dissatisfaction among PhD students have been a defining characteristic of doctoral education. Researchers are increasingly concerned about the high number of PhD candidates who fail to graduate as dropping out can have numerous negative consequences on PhD students (Levecque et al., 2017). Attrition rates support this notion: 33–70% of those who start their PhD never finish (Jones, 2013). Also, Castelló et al., (2017) revealed that one-third of a sample of doctoral students who were still enrolled had at some point intended to dropout.

High doctoral dropout rates challenge universities both competitively and financially because a large share of their research output depends on PhD students (Horta et al., 2018).

Almost universally, residential doctoral programs have reported attrition rates of up to 50% and nearly 50-70% for online doctoral programs (Terrell et al., 2012), and this loss of potential doctorates has limited applicants for positions requiring a doctorate and depleted resources from universities and students (Willis & Carmichael, 2011). Attrition rates for doctoral students have been reported to be as high as 50% (Brill, 2014). Of those students who do graduate from their lengthy doctoral program, approximately 50% of students who start do not finish (Council of Graduate School [CGS], 2012). In addition, those who strive to finish their doctoral program, do so at a considerably longer time than the time slot for PhD. Of the total students who do persist in a doctoral program, 41% complete their degree program within 7 years, while 57% take up to 10 years to complete their degree (Ampaw & Jaeger, 2011, p. 640). According to the CGS (as cited in Ampaw & Jaeger, 2011), nationwide databases are not maintained on attrition rates of doctoral students; records are only kept for those who graduate.

Aside the general approximation regarding PhD dropout rate, the numbers vary quite a bit in terms of different program styles, university by university standards, as well as differences in discipline. In the US for instance, attrition rates for PhD programs across the fields of engineering, life sciences,

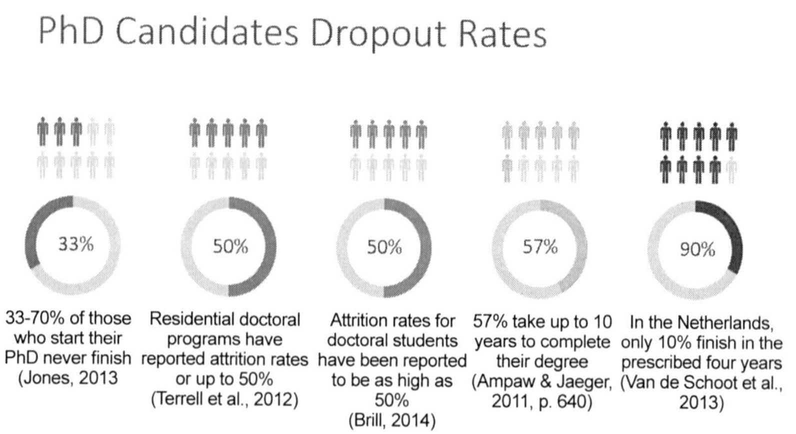

Figure 1: PhD Candidates Dropout Rates

mathematics and physical sciences, and humanities range from 36 – 51% (Young et al., 2019). In the UK, the PhD failure rate is 19.5% with 16.2% of students leaving their PhD program early (DiscoverPhDs, 2019). In the Netherlands, only 10% manage to finish in the commonly prescribed four years and the average completion time is five years (Van de Schoot et al., 2013). While in Hungary, statistics show that two fifths of bachelor's students, one fifth of master's students, and half of doctoral students leave higher education without earning their degree (Derényi, 2015).

2. Factors for Attrition of PhD Students

Reported reasons for attrition include personal issues, the nature of the doctoral program, financial considerations, emotional stress, and family obligations (Gregoric & Wilson, 2012; Holmes et al., 2010). Factors such as individual's psychological characteristics, student's behaviour, family background, sociological and social aspects, pedagogical–psychological factors, institutional structure, institutional resources, etc., can be mentioned (Bocsi et al., 2018).

Individual characteristics were also identified as factors that affected attrition and persistence in doctoral programs (Spaulding & Rockinson-Szapkiw, 2012; Van de Schoot et al., 2013). For example, married students had a higher retention rate than unmarried students and as age increased, the probability of dropping out decreased (Lott et al., 2010). Thus, many of the factors that enhanced persistence or engendered attrition in doctoral programs were quite individual and unique characteristics of each candidate (Lott et al., 2010; Spaulding & Rockinson-Szapkiw, 2012; Van de Schoot et al., 2013).

A positive and non-hierarchical relationship between the doctoral committee chair and the doctoral candidate has been identified as one of the most critical factors in the successful completion of a doctorate degree (Bitzer, 2011; Stallone, 2011; Storms et al., 2011). However, only 26 of 457 (6%) candidate respondents identified their supervisor in a positive light (Bégin & Gérard, 2013) and when surveyed, doctoral students repeatedly identified the most consistent and significant barrier to their success in the degree program was a problematic relationship with the dissertation chair (Willis & Carmichael, 2011).

Time management is also a factor responsible for the high attrition rate of PhD students. Martinez et al. (2013) found that four out of five doctoral students identified time management as the greatest challenge in their doctoral program. West et al. (2011) research indicated that of the participants interviewed, 60% found time management and balancing life obligations challenging for doctoral students. Ford and Vaughn (2011) indicated students face family conflicts because of the hours needed to complete the doctoral program.

In the PhD journey, a positive and effective relationship between PhD students and their supervisors is paramount to their success (Ali et al., 2016). The most important relationship for a

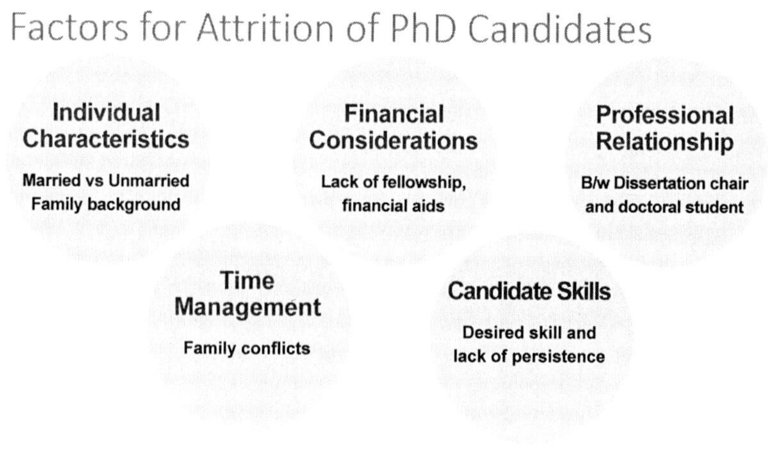

Figure 2: Factors for Attrition of PhD Candidates

doctoral student is with an advisor, faculty, or chairperson (Holley & Caldwell, 2012). Another study conducted by Devos et al., (2016) took a qualitative approach into comparing, completing, and departing doctoral students. Interviews with 21 former doctoral students showed that while support from doctoral peers played a positive role in the doctoral process for all students, it was not enough to sustain a sense of belonging and by consequence persistence towards degree completion. Students described doctoral advisor support, particularly as they increased student's self-efficacy and belongingness, as the distinguishing factor that kept departing students from degree completion.

Lack of candidate's ability or skills were identified as critical reasons why candidates failed to complete their degree (Herman, 2011; Kyvik & Olsen, 2014); thus, prior academic preparation was deemed a major factor in persistence (Ampaw & Jaeger, 2011). Often doctoral candidates did not understand that success in doctoral studies required a different skill set than what they previously possessed (Brill et al., 2014). Candidates with certain skills and preparation were found to be more likely to persist than those without these skills and preparation factors that influenced degree completion may be categorized as motivation, psychological, prior academic preparation, program preparation, and demographics (Bitzer, 2011; Brill et al., 2014; Mason, 2012; Stock & Siegfried, 2014).

There is an abundance of existing literature on the relationship that exists between a supervisor and doctoral student. However, not much has been researched about how effective supervisory styles are to each student. While confirming that good academic relationships between supervisors and PhD students were associated with student's satisfaction (Erichsen et al., 2014), existing literatures hasn't tested the effectiveness of supervisory style adopted by the supervisor to each student. Most of the supervisors tend to use a particular style on all students without taking into consideration the different levels of learners where some are considered slow, fast, and intermediate learners. In supervision, there is no one-size-fits-all model and this makes it necessary for supervisors to know their strengths and weaknesses in order to determine how best to support doctoral students. As postulated by McIntosh (2016), the process of evaluating one's own supervisory style can make faculty more effective supervisors. Research across North America has consistently shown that effective supervision and mentorship are the most important features of a student's graduate school experience, and indeed are major factors in driving program completion or attrition (CGS, 2009).

In education, the concept of student engagement typically arises when there is a high-level prioritization of educational, teaching, and relational techniques by educators that focuses on the intellectual, developmental, behavioral, social, physical, and emotional factors which either enhances or undermines students' learning (Iroegbu & Agboola, 2019). Holley and Caldwell (2012) found that students in doctoral programs were more likely to complete their program and experience greater satisfaction when they were engaged in meaningful interaction with the advisor. Research by Ewing, Mathieson, Alexander, and Leafman (2012, p. 40) indicated that a doctoral program with intense facilitation and dialogue can increase the graduation rate upto 73%.

Financial incapability is also a major reason for the high rate of doctoral students' dropout. Students who are awarded a fellowship have higher completion rates than students who are awarded an assistantship or who are totally self-supporting (Ampaw & Jaeger, 2011). Kim and Otts (2010) found that students who paid for their degree incrementally, without other support, were more likely to not complete or took longer (see also Gardner, 2010; Offerman, 2011). Conversely, doctoral students who had financial support in the form of research assistantships (Stock & Siegfried, 2014), scholarships (Jiranek, 2010), or financial aid, were more likely to persist (Bitzer, 2011; Holly & Caldwell, 2012; West et al., 2011).

The quality of academic interaction and supervision between a doctoral student and supervisor has also been touted to be responsible for the successful completion of PhD. Take for instance, Basturkmen et al., (2014) posited that social support and interaction that PhD students have with their supervisors are proved to contribute greatly to their study completion. This notion was supported by Hamid and Shah (2018) who emphasized the necessity to have healthy academic interactions between supervisors and research scholars in order to ensure the successful completion of research projects. Lott et al., (2010) who posited doctoral students may leave the doctoral program due to a lack of socialization, especially those who are relatively isolated demographically. Martinez et al., (2013) noted doctoral students typically did not leave the program for one reason but chose to leave due to multiple factors that included support and isolation.

Research indicated that doctoral mentoring programs in which the instructor provided additional time for students outside of the classroom environment to meet student needs, led to successful student learning (Yob & Crawford, 2012). Rockinson-Szapkiw et al., (2014) noted online doctoral students who used web-based technologies for communication had a higher sense of connectedness than doctoral students who used the phone or email, and results highlighted how web-based communication tools can increase connectedness and decrease doctoral attrition.

❒

Chapter 2
Factors for College Dropout

According to Thinkimpact (2021), 40% of students' dropout of college every year in the USA. 30% of students dropout in the first year. Only 41% of students graduate in 4 years. Male students have a 20% higher chance to dropout than female students.

- 38% of college students' dropout due to financial shortcomings for their college education.
- 13% of the students find it hard to fit into the social life at college.
- The lack of adequate support from the family contributes to 90% of college dropouts.
- 28% of college students' dropout due to academic disqualification – failure to meet the set academic requirements.
- Mental, emotional, or psychological issues cause 3% of college students to dropout.
- Students who live far away from their college eventually dropout because of the distance. This is responsible for 4% of the college dropouts.
- 5% of the students who dropout cite health problems as the main reason for dropping out of college.
- 89% of students from the first generation in low earning families tend to dropout of college.

Comparing Dropout Rate Among Different Educational Levels

Researches on dropout among participants with different educational levels are scantily reported. Although some studies revealed that people with a lower educational level have higher dropout rates than highly educated people (Geraghty et al., 2013; Price et al., 2012; Murray et al., 2013), other studies did not find educational differences in terms of dropout (Peels et al., 2012; Ezendam et al., 2014; Habibovic et al., 2014). This may be attributed to the fact that people with lower educational level are known to indulge in unhealthy lifestyle such as use of tobacco (Hiscock et al., 2012; Savage, 2012; Grittner et al., 2013) unhealthy quantities of alcohol absorption (Groot & Maassen van den Brink, 2006), eating less vegetables (Hulshof, 2003), are less physically active (Vlismas, 2009) and have a higher likelihood of being obese (Cutler & Lleras-Muney, 2010). This is supported by a study conducted by Reinward et al., (2015) who concluded that dropout attrition rates were higher among participants with a lower or middle educational level compared with highly educational participants.

Henderson (2020) gave the following dropout rates for higher education; community college: 61%; Bachelor's degree: 45%; Master's degree: 39% and PhD: 50%. Henderson (2020) further stated that in California, the dropout rate for community college is 70% and that only 30% manage to obtain a degree or transfer to a four-year college, while only 55% of those studying for a bachelor's degree actually graduated. Despite students' investments of time and energy, approximately 50% of students do not complete a doctoral degree they begin (Cassuto, 2013).

Gates (2017) in a blog post titled "putting students first" said that college dropout rates needed to be addressed as the US has the highest college dropout rate. Gates (2017) went further to say that though it was great that more than 2 million American students will start college that fall "Based on the latest college completion trends, only about half of all those students (54.8%) will leave college with a diploma. The rest - most of them low - income, first generation, and minority students - will not finish a degree. They'll dropout."

The first phase of Bachelors', Masters', and PhD program is the coursework and it is a familiar phase for all educational levels, therefore does not pose much of a problem since most students can conveniently scale through it even though it is just a couple of months for Master and may take two or three years for PhD. The second phase is the most crucial for PhD students and here lies the problematic phase. West et al., (2011) declared that the second stage which includes the self-directed dissertation development and research phases, is unfamiliar territory for most doctoral students. In the dissertation phase, students often work alone with only occasional interaction with their advisor or faculty member, and many schools do not promote interaction among students (Ali & Kohun, 2006). This isolation can lead to self-doubt about student progress and the ability to finish the dissertation (Ali & Kohun, 2006). Students may find themselves distressed during a doctoral program, which can cause them to withdraw from the academic community (Pyhalto et al., 2012). This is majorly the phase where most doctoral students' dropout.

❒

Chapter 3

Research Methods Used to Study Attrition Data and Analysis

Rooij et al., (2021) conducted a study to investigate which supervision, psychosocial, and project characteristics are related to satisfaction, progress, and quit intentions in a sample of 839 PhD candidates at a university in the Netherlands.

Method: Hierarchical Multiple Regression Analyses

Instrument: The study used items from questionnaires that have been validated and used in previous studies. It was pilot tested by 16 PhD students who thought aloud while completing it.

Result: Experienced workload was negatively related to satisfaction and progress, and positively to quit intentions. The quality of the supervisor-PhD candidate relationship, the PhD candidate's sense of belonging, the amount of freedom in the project, and working on a project closely related to the supervisor's research were positively related to satisfaction and negatively to quit intentions.

Table 1. Measurement characteristics of the variables used in this study.

Factor	Sample Items	Number of Items	Cronbach's Alpha
Dependent variables			
Satisfaction	Overall, how satisfied are you with your PhD trajectory? (5-point scale: 'very dissatisfied' – 'very satisfied')	1	-
Progress	Are you currently on schedule with your work? (4-point scale: 'No, I have fallen very far behind and won't be able to finish in time' – 'Yes, I think I will be able to finish in time')	1	-
Intention to quit	Have you ever considered quitting your PhD project? (4-point scale: 'no, never' 'yes, very often')	1	-
Supervision characteristics			
Autonomy support	My supervisor provides me with choices and options.	8	.81
Personal support	My supervisor expresses understanding and empathy when I experience difficulties.	13	.96
Academic support	My supervisor helps me to plan and manage the different research tasks I have to complete.	10	.92
Availability	My supervisor responds to my queries or requests for help within a reasonable time frame.	3	.85
High expectations	My supervisor expects me to publish in high-impact journals.	6	.70
Relationship	Overall, how would you describe your relationship with your supervisor? (5-point scale: 'very bad' – 'very good')	1	-
Psychosocial factors			
Academic relationships	Colleagues approach me to discuss their work.	8	.87
Social relationships	I regularly spend time outside work with my colleagues.	4	.85
Sense of belonging	I enjoy the atmosphere in my department.	5	.91
Project characteristics			
Freedom	I have the freedom to make my own choices about the direction of my project and the methods to be used.	6	.81
Workload	How would you describe the workload in your PhD project? (5-point scale: 'too high' – 'too low')	1	-
Stand-alone project	Is your project a stand-alone project, i.e., are you the only one working on that topic? ('yes' or 'no')	1	-

Project with close link to supervisor's research	Is your project closely linked to your supervisor's research? ('yes' or 'no')	1	-
Teaching tasks	Do you teach and/or supervise students? ('yes' or 'no')	1	-

Source: Rooij et al., (2021).

Table 1 provides an overview of all factors including sample items, number of items, and reliabilities. The supervisor support scales, i.e., autonomy support, personal support, academic support, and supervisor availability, were based on scales developed by Overall, Deane, and Peterson (2011). The scales regarding psychosocial factors – formal relationships, informal relationships, and sense of belonging – were based on scales that Meeuwisse, Severiens, and Born (2010) used in a study of undergraduate students.

Table 2. Descriptive Statistics: Means, standard deviations, and ranges

Variable	M	SD	Range
Dependent variables			
Satisfaction	3.72	.88	1–5
Progress	3.19	1.04	1-4
Intention to quit	1.40	.72	1-4
Supervision characteristics			
Academic support	3.68	.81	1-5
Personal support	4.02	.76	1-5
Autonomy support	4.06	.57	1-5
Availability	4.32	.76	1-5
High expectations	2.75	.60	1-5
Relationship	4.44	.74	1-5
Psychosocial factors			
Academic integration	3.61	.65	1.25-5
Social integration	3.53	.80	1-5
Sense of belonging	3.87	.71	1-5
Project characteristics			
Freedom	3.95	.62	1.67-5
Workload	3.59	.63	1-5
Stand-alone project	.50	.50	0-1
Project with close link to supervisor's research	.40	.49	0-1
Teaching tasks	.70	.46	0-1

Source: Rooij et al., (2021).

In Table 2, Means, standard deviations, and ranges of all variables are displayed.

Table 3. Descriptive statistics: Answers on the questions regarding being on schedule and considering quitting.

Are you currently on schedule with your work?	I was unable to finish in time and am currently on an extension or finishing my thesis in my own time.	No, I have fallen behind and I don't think I will be able to finish in time	No, I have fallen behind, but I still think I will be able to finish in time.	Yes, I think I will be able to finish in time.
%	11.1	12.5	22.6	53.8
Have you ever considered quitting your PhD project?	Yes, very often	Yes, often	Yes, sometimes	No, never
%	3.3	3.8	22.5	70.3

Source: Rooij et al., (2021).

In Table 3, percentages are shown regarding PhD candidates' expectations to finish in time and how often they had considered quitting the PhD.

In a study, Wollast et al., (2018) analyzed the population of doctoral students in all disciplines of the two largest universities of the French-speaking Community of Belgium (N = 1509). Specifically, the study focused on several factors: gender, nationality, marital status, master grade, whether students continued at the same university when transitioning to the doctoral degree, whether they continued in the same field, age at registration, research field and funding (i.e., type of funding and associated job requirements).

Method: Logistic regression analyses, multiple logistic regression analysis

Instrument: Questionnaires and data from the administrative databases of both universities.

Result: Findings indicate that four factors (marital status, master grade, research field and funding) are directly associated with dropout rate when all factors are considered jointly in the same model. In addition, result found that an accumulation of risk factors leads to a massive increase in dropout rates. Finally, a time course analysis revealed that the highest dropout rate occurs during the first two years and is related to the absence of funding or scholarship.

Table 4: Rates of doctoral completion and dropout within a period of 8 years

	Frequency	**Percent**
Success	820	54.3%
Probably dropped out	572	37.9%
Probably still active	117	7.8%
Total	1509	100%

Source: Wollast et al., (2018).

Table 4 presents the number of PhD students depending on whether they succeeded, dropped out or were still active within a period of eight years.

Table 5. Success rates as a function of factors

	Frequency	Success rate		Frequency	Success rate
Gender			*Marital status*		
Male	779	60.6%	Married	376	67.3%
Female	613	50.8%	Unmarried	946	53.7%
Nationality			*Age*		
Belgian nationals	841	62.5%	Lower than 26 years old	669	65.6%
Nationals from another EU country	255	56.9%	Between 26 and 40 years old	637	55.1%
Non-EU nationals	296	50.3%	Higher than 40 years old	86	34.9%
Master grade			*Research field*		

Summa cum laude	150	81.3%	Science and technologies	555	68.6%
Magna cum laude	456	62.1%	Health sciences	362	49.4%
Cum laude	256	49.2%	Social sciences	362	49.4%
Success without honors	26	34.6%	Humanities	197	48.2%
University			*Field*		
Same university	745	62%	Same field	1064	61%
Different university	616	56%	Different field	281	54.8%
Finding					
Fellowship	351	80.1%	Research grant	308	64%
Assistantship	170	67.6%	No- or unknown funding	563	4.03%

Source: Wollast et al., (2018).

Table 5 aggregates success rates as a function of each factor.

Table 6. Prediction of doctoral success/dropout for all variables

Variables	**β**	**Standard Deviation**	**Wald**	**Degree of freedom**	**P value**	**OR**
Nationality ("Belgian nationals" versus "non-EU nationals")	-.28	.45	.38	1	.54	.76
Marital status	**-1.47**	**.22**	**44.01**	**1**	**.00**	**.23**
Master grade ("high distinction" versus "satisfaction")	-.32	.52	.39	1	.53	.72
Master grade ("high distinction" versus "distinction")	-.22	.20	1.26	1	.26	.80
Master grade ("high distinction" versus "very high distinction")	**.92**	**.26**	**12.31**	**1**	**.00**	**2.50**

Change of university between undergraduate and doctoral degree	-.16	.23	.51	1	.48	.85
Age at registration ("less than 26 years old" versus "between 26 and 40 years old")	.22	.21	1.13	1	.29	1.25
Age at registration ("less than 26 years old" versus "strictly more than 40 years old")	-.80	.48	2.77	1	.10	.45
Research field ("science and technology" versus "humanities")	**-.73**	**.26**	**8.13**	**1**	**.00**	**.48**
Research field ("sciences and technologies" versus "social sciences")	-.20	.22	.78	1	.38	.82
Research field ("science and technology" versus "health sciences")	-.08	.23	.13	1	.72	.92
Funding ("no-funding or unknown funding" versus "assistant lectureship")	**1.09**	**.26**	**17.07**	**1**	**.00**	**2.96**
Funding ("no-funding or unknown funding" versus "non-university funding")	**1.80**	**.26**	**48.24**	**1**	**.00**	**6.06**
Funding ("no-funding or unknown funding" versus "research project")	**.78**	**.24**	**10.49**	**1**	**.00**	**2.19**
Constant	.70	.31	5.09	1	.02	2.01

Source: Wollast et al., (2018).

Table 6 presents the results of this multivariate analysis. These results show that four factors (marital status, master grade, research field and funding) are directly associated with dropout rate when all factors are considered together in the same model (Note 2).

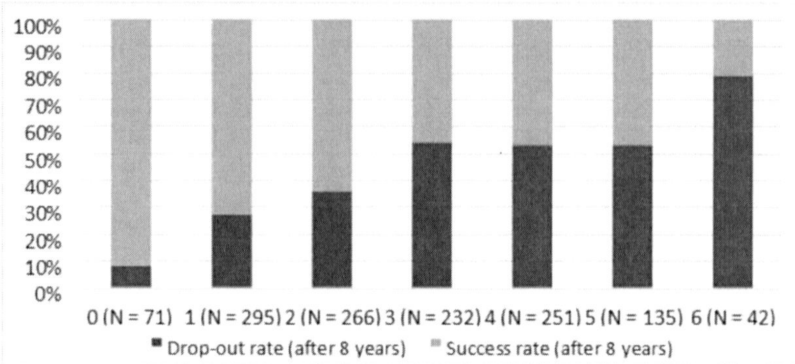

Figure 3: Success and drop-out rates as a function of the number of risk factors accumulated

In Figure 3, it was observed that the highest success rate (92%) was when there were zero risk factors and the highest dropout rate (79%) when six risks had been accumulated. More importantly, the results show a linear progression of dropout rates as a function of risk factors accumulated with an increase until three years plus a peak at three and six risks.

Scott (2010) conducted an exploratory study of first-semester student attrition in a community college to determine if student's background variables (age, gender, race, academic preparation); student status (part/full-time student), and student's circumstances (commuting distance, independent/dependent financial student status) could predict fall-to-spring attrition (2006-2007) in a sample of 542 first-time, first-semester students at a community college in Southern Indiana. This study also included the results from an exit survey administered in the spring semester by the college. The sample consisted of 403 students who persisted to the next semester, and 121 students who did not persist to the next semester.

Method: Descriptive statistics, Hierarchical logistic regression, and exit survey analysis.

Instrument: Data provided by the college's enrolment database, and a college-administered exit survey.

Result: The students who persisted to the second semester were slightly older and had a higher percentage of males. The students who did not persist to the second semester had higher percentages of females and higher percentages of minority students and students with entrance scores requiring remedial classes before taking program specific classes. Results of the hierarchical logistic regression indicated the COMPASS reading score variable and the full-and part-time student status variable were statistically significant predictors of attrition.

Table 7: A comparison of persisters (n = 403), non-persisters (n = 121), and college population

Variable	Persisters	Non-persisiters	Population
Percentage of sample	77%	23%	
Mean Age	24.9	23.7	28.6
Females	42%	51%	52%
Males	58%	49%	48%
White	90%	84%	84%
Black	6%	10%	5%
Program Ready: Reading	65%	39%	---
Program Ready: Math	58%	42%	---
Mean Driving Distance	31.6 miles	22.8 miles	---
Independent	63%	57%	---
Dependent	37%	43%	---

Source: Scott (2010). *Note*: Dashes indicate data not provided by college.

Table 7 presents a comparison of first-time first semester students who persisted to the next semester and the students that did not persist by gender, race, academic readiness, driving distances, and independent/dependent student status. In table 7, there was no statistical difference for age between persisters and non-persisters; but the mean age for both groups was close. Black students were a higher percentage of the non-persisting group than the persisting group. Persisters had higher percentages of program ready students in reading and math than non-persisters. A higher percentage of independent students were persisters (63%) than non-persisters (57%), and independent students were the majority in both groups. For driving distance, students that persisted drove more miles than those that did not persist.

Table 8: Question 5, Exit Survey Demographics

	Lives alone	Lives with parents	Lives with other relatives	Lives with spouse or partner	Lives with students or frien	Full-time course load	Part-time course load	23 years of age or younger	24 years of age or old
Males (n=24)	3	7	0	13	1	7	17	5	19
Females (n=57)	12	10	2	33	0	11	46	17	40
Total *N*=81	15	17	2	46	1	18	63	22	59

Source: Scott (2010).

The data for Table 8 were condensed from the actual survey responses. Living arrangements, student course load, and age are shown in the table, with a total of 81 respondents. Female respondents were the majority. For males, three lived alone, seven lived with parents, 13 lived with a spouse or partner, and one lived with a friend. 17 males attended part-time, and 7 males attended full-time. 19 males were 24 or older, and 5 males were 23 or younger. For female students, 12 lived alone, 10 lived with parents, 2 lived with relatives, 33 lived with a spouse or partner, 1 lived with a friend, and 46 females attended part-time. More respondents lived with a spouse or partner (46). Of the total respondents that lived with a spouse or partner, the majority were female (33), and more respondents attended part-time (63) than full-time (18). Females composed the majority of the part-time student respondents (46). The mean age of the survey sample was 31.5. More female respondents were over 24 (40).

Table 9: *Question 5, Exit Survey Results-Q. 9, N* = 81 respondents

	n	**% of sample**	**Female**	**Male**	**Full-time status**	**Part-time status**
What are you doing now?						
Work full-time	46	57.5%	30	16	7	39
Caring for children or other family	23	28.3%	21	2	6	17
Work part-time	15	18.5%	13	2	5	10
Other	15	18.5%	9	6	5	10
Registered at another institution	11	13.6%	7	4	5	6
Other family obligations	11	13.6%	8	2	2	8
Not working	9	11.1%	5	4	2	7

Source: Scott (2010).

Survey question 9 asked: "What are you doing now?" Table 9 shows the number of students for each question's choice of response, the percentage of the sample represented by the response, the gender of the respondent, and the enrollment status (full-time and part-time) of the student. From Table 9, the majority of the respondents (46) indicated they were *working full-time*, and accounted for almost 58% of the sample. Of the total students who worked full-time, 39 respondents carried a part-time course load, and seven carried a full-time course load. The next highest response is *caring for children* (23), and as expected, most of the respondents were female (21). 17 of the students that cared for children attended college part-time, and 6 students attended full-time. *Working part-time* and *other* had the same percentage of the sample, 18.5%. 13 females and 2 males worked part-time, and 10 of the 15 students working part-time also attended college part-time. For the category *other*, 9 students were female and 6 were male. 10 of the students in the other category attended part-time. *Registered at another institution* and *other family obligations* had the same number of respondents at eleven, respectively. 7 of the students that transferred were female and 4 were male. 5 students attended full-time and 6 attended part-time. For *other family obligations*, 8 of the students were female and 2 were male, two students were full-time students and 8 were part-time students. *Caring for children* and *other family obligations* together accounted for about 42% of the respondents. When *working full-time* was added in, these three categories accounted for over 85% of the respondents.

Table 10: *Question 5, Exit Survey Results-Q. 10, N* = 81 respondents

	n	% of sample	Female	Male	Full-time status	Part-time status
Why did you leave?						
Financial difficulty	26	32.0%	8	18	4	22
Family obligations	22	27.1%	19	3	5	17
Illness	15	18.5%	7	8	4	11
Employment (needed to work)	15	18.5%	10	5	3	12
Registered at another school	11	13.6%	7	4	4	7
Unsure if program meets goals	7	8.6%	4	3	0	7
Dissatisfied with program	5	6.2%	4	1	1	4
Dissatisfied with quality of instruction	5	6.2%	5	0	1	4
Lack of interest	4	4.9%	3	1	2	2
Dissatisfied with student services	3	3.7%	3	0	0	3
Dissatisfied with facilities	3	3.7%	2	1	2	2
Moved to another city/state	1	1.2%	1	0	0	1

Source: Scott (2010).

Table 10 shows the choices and responses for the exit survey question 10. The table shows the number of students for each question's choice of response, the percentage of the sample represented by the response, the respondent's gender, and the enrolment status (full-time and part-time) of the student. The top response was *financial difficulties* (26). This represented 32% of the responses. Of this category, 18 were male and 8 were female. 22 students attended part-time and 4 attended full-time. The next highest response in rank was *family obligations* (22), and this category represented 27.1% of the responses. Of this category, 19 students were female, and 3 were male. 17 students attended part-time and 5 attended full-time. *Employment and illness* tied for third highest with 15 responses respectively. Each of the two categories represented 18.5% of the sample. For *employment*, 10 students were female, and 5 were male. 12 students attended part-time and 3 attended full-time. For *illness*, 7 students were female, and 8 were male. 11 students attended part-time and 4 attended full-time.

Summary

The research methods used in this study were from the research carried out by Rooij et al., (2021); Wollast et al., (2018); and Scott (2010). Firstly, in the study conducted by Rooij et al., (2012), descriptive statistics were used to display all variables, and hierarchical multiple regression analysis was used to assess the impact of supervision characteristics, psychosocial factors, and project characteristics on satisfaction, progress, and intention to quit. Secondly, Wollast et al., (2018) carried out a study using prevalence analysis to present rates of doctoral completion and dropout within a period of 8 years; univariate logistic regression analysis with the coded contrast was used to separately study the factors associated with success and dropout; multiple logistic regression analysis was used in an attempt to obtain a model that identifies factors that, when taken together, may tend to predict successful submission; and time course analysis was used as a function of funding among PhD students who dropped out. Lastly, Scott (2010) carried out an exploratory study to determine if student's background variables, status and circumstances could predict fall-to-spring attrition. Here, descriptive statistics were used to identify differences between persisters and non-persisters; hierarchical logistic regression was used to determine which study variables best predicted second semester student attrition; and the exit survey analysis was used to provide anecdotal snapshots of student attrition.

Conclusion and Recommendations

This article made an attempt to examine the various reasons responsible for the high rate of dropouts in all educational levels most especially doctoral programs where it is obvious that there is a plethora of factors that contributes to this menace. It is a known fact though students are responsible for their level of preparedness and commitment to task, the university also has a big role to play especially in the areas of providing students with accountable and qualified advisors, and creating an enabling environment. On the part of the lecturers and professors, ensuring multidimensional and varied support to students is also vital. Overtime, this is assured to facilitate students' persistence and completion. It is therefore recommended that, at the start of a new PhD journey, students and advisors should have clear and candid discussions about guidelines, targets, activities, responsibilities' and struggles that will be experienced as this is crucial to the development of trust between both parties. Also, the PhD students having high and rigorous workload should be revisited and critically examined as this will help mitigate against the high dropout rate.

❐

Chapter 4

Successful Strategy in Choosing a Research Topic and Completing PhD

Introduction

Anyone can do a PhD, not necessarily a brilliant person but someonc who is basically ready to put in the much-needed effort, persist, and manage his/her time well. Practically, it entails making up one's mind to give up a significant chunk of one's life for a particular period of time in order to accomplish something where thc rcward is mostly personal. PhD completion can be accomplished if one is motivated by personal reward rather than being motivated by the values of one's social group. Lindley et al (2020) stated that while students with varying mindset have the potential to complete PhD across all groups, those with clearly stated personal goals appear to make the best progress. Most people regard PhD as a mystical goal that can only be achieved by a special group of people, but it is actually a social and academic construct that can only be achieved with the right amount of intelligence, determination, commitment and resilience. The most significant factor in the timeliness and quality of completion is a student's self-belief that they are progressing through the program (Devos et al., 2017).

Core Attributes Required to Complete a PhD

While it is my firm belief that anyone can start and complete a PhD degree, it is also true that it would require them to have or develop certain traits in order to do so. These qualities will allow them to effectively and effortlessly undergo the whole process.

1. Intellectual curiosity

One of the most valued qualities that every PhD aspirant needs to develop is intellectual curiosity. An inquisitive mind that constantly asks questions like why and how. One should have insatiable hungry for knowledge and a drive to solve complex problem. It is must for a PhD student to demonstrate a willingness and ability to learn new things with an open mind and flexibility towards unconventional and alternate answers. Top grades cannot solely make for a good PhD students, it is the willingness to turn one's curiosity into a dedicated course of study that makes for a successful PhD candidate. It is possible that intellectual curiosity doesn't come naturally and may require some effort. However, with simple steps this too can become a personality trait. Here are some ways you can pique your intellectual curiosity:

- **Ask questions, even if they seem silly:** At the core of learning is asking questions about everything. Only when you ask question, then only you completely understand a topic, issue or concept at hand. Asking questions may feel unnatural or unintelligent at first. However, this is the first step towards discovering new things and gaining knowledge. Furthermore, it will allow us to learn more about the subject and clarify any misconceptions or false knowledge that might have existed in our minds.
- **Acknowledge the gap in your knowledge:** We are often afraid to admit that we don't know something because

we are embarrassed about it. Learning to admit that there is a gap in our knowledge can provide us the opportunity to learn something new. It is when we let the gap be that our curiosity is stagnated. A knowledge gap is an opportunity to learn.

- **Follow your interest but also diversify:** There are topics that we are interested in and are passionate about. But do we know everything there is to know about it? Probably not. Therefore it is good idca to follow one's own interests with the purpose to understand it deeply. Redirecting our attention to explore unchartered territory of the topic of interest might open a new avenue of knowledge. It is equally important to explore and diversify into related topics to see if that piques our interest. In this way we'll learn about newer things and also grow our information base.
- **Talk to people:** People are moving encyclopedias of knowledge. Talking to peers as well as scholars in different fields gives the opportunity to broaden our horizon and accumulate information about different topics that might be of interest to us. It opens our eyes to different sides of things which we may have been previously unaware.

Inculcating intellectual curiosity will lead to generation of original ideas, nuanced thinking and better problem solving which are instrumental in a PhD program.

2. Intelligence

A PhD student is always expected to display high level of intelligence. True as it may be, it is not just intellect that plays a part but simple traits like common sense, academic ability and brightness that can make all the difference.

In order to pursue a challenging program like PhD, one must be intelligent enough to identify and pursue a PhD in an area/ field where one has a level of competence and interest in. More often than not, students are completely confused and unclear about the area of interest. A major myth about doctoral studies is that they must invent great ideas. While there have been people with PhDs have made ground breaking discoveries but rarely does this happen during their time of study. Overwhelmed by this idea, many have made the mistake of choosing an overambitious topic that they are not completely confident about nor are they interested in. When they choose such a subject they are setting themselves up for failure. Sooner or later, they are faced with challenges that they then are unable to tackle leading to distress and disappointment.

This is where intelligence comes to play. It is those who assess their core competence and use it to work smartly and independently are able to conduct high quality research and present their findings in clear prose. Remember, PhD is not about a single never been done before topic or one great idea. Instead, it is about intelligently choosing a topic that would add to already existing body of knowledge.

3. Resilience

With a program of this intensity, the quality that comes handy the most is resilience. There will be times when one will be challenged and even feel disillusioned but it is important to remember to stay the course with irrational ambition. A PhD student must be resilient enough to interrogate a problem with a focused mind and unwavering faith in one's capability.

Quite often students find it challenging to accept constructive feedback. They feel flattened with feelings of shame, inadequacy, and fear of failure. These complex negative emotions often hinder their progress and even derail them from their path. Learning to positively take all kinds of feedback is important in order to be resilient. Another issue that some PhD students face is lack of resilience in resource gathering. In the chapter on literature review where credible and published research work must be included, students are unable to cite from sources that are verifiable or even relevant. This becomes a major pressure points for them and often struggle with it. In such a case, it is easy to want to give up and compromise of the quality or entirely give up. It helps to remember that unless your topic is in an extremely niche area of study, there are plenty of resources available, both online and offline. Google Scholar is your first stop in resource gathering and one must always go beyond page 5 of the results. Take some time out to meet with your supervisor, peers, and librarians to understand the process and work through it. Everything gets better with time and so will your skill in gathering relevant resources. There will be struggles attaining a PhD, especially to deal with the complexities of the subject and the program. This is bound to challenge you and raise questions in your mind but you must learn to build researcher resilience.

There are no shortcuts to success. Only hard work and diligence can help achieve one's goal, no matter how difficult they may seem. One must learn to push through the rough patches, confusion, disappointments, lost information, and failure of well-planned projects. Enduring through these challenges will make you stronger and resilient.

4. Patience

Patience is a virtue that every PhD aspirant must possess. Patience is the quality of waiting calmly and not giving up when things appear to get hard. It is the ability to face disappointments and still continue to work hard to accomplish one's goals. Conducting research is a time consuming and challenging task, which will test you at every step. Right from the onset of the program—whether it is choosing a topic and selecting the right supervisor or acquiring funding for your study—you will face many big and small hurdles.

Every researcher, especially a PhD student, must inculcate the quality of patience and not give into ones frustration. One should have the ability and determination to take challenges in life and be prepared to face failures without losing hope. Impatience leads to poor performance and impacts one's mental and physical health, which further disrupts the course of action. Impatience creates further problem. It can be quite difficult to work with people but impatient people make it twice as hard. Only when one learns to be patient does one find true satisfaction in any task. Persevering through difficult situations, failures, and rejections can be hard but not impossible.

Not everyone is born with this virtue but there are ways that can help build patience:

- **Reassess the situation:** Often becoming impatient is linked with one's ideologies and belief systems. When situation that doesn't align with our beliefs, we tend to lose control of our emotions. For instance, if you are extremely punctual but your peers are always late for meetings, it is natural to have a negative react. However, one can also see this as an opportunity to either get some reading done or just enjoy a few minutes to themselves. Patience is connected to self-control, and conscious effort to regulate one's emotions. It is can help in training our self-control.
- **Identify frequent triggers:** When faced with a frustrating situation, often students waste all their energy in venting their anger. While that may seem like a fair response, it is a futile activity. It only worsens

the situation and impacts you and your relationships negatively. Identifying triggers can help contain one's reaction. Every time you are faced with a situation and you can sense the impending reaction, take a step back and don't engage with that emotion. Practising this can significantly improve your patience levels and prevent a negative outburst of anger.

- **Practice mindfulness:** As clichéd as it may sound, practising mindfulness in the form of meditation, deep breathing, and reflecting on your emotions really helps in emotion management and patience. Taking some time out to meditate or a few long and deep breaths can help change in one's emotions drastically. Observing this change in emotion can help to react with more patience.

Like the Chinese proverb rightly points out, "One moment of patience may ward off great disaster. One moment of impatience may ruin a whole life."

For many PhD students, a bit of patience is all it takes to succeed and complete the program.

5. Problem solving ability and creativity

PhD is not simply a research-driven program. It requires one to think objectively as well as creatively. The ability to think in terms of facts, evidences, and numbers but at the same time think imaginatively and creatively in order to find solutions and answers in a unique manner. It requires one to be willing to take a chance and try methods that are out of the box or even unattempted.

Every PhD student must possess problem solving skill since a major portion of their time will be spent in juggling between finding solutions for academic problems and real-life problems. Therefore, developing solving skills becomes essential. It requires one to expand their knowledge and approach in keeping with problem solving processes. The process includes asking a set of basic questions like:

- ✓ What is the problem?
- ✓ What are the causes of the said problem?
- ✓ What are the potential alternatives to the problem?
- ✓ Which alternative should be applied?

By asking such questions, one becomes aware of the various elements of the problem. This may also be an opportunity to look and assess things differently, and thereby developing a creative solution. Problem solving skill, can be developed and honed quite easily. Here are some ways one can improve their problem solving skill

- **Understand the problem:** The first step to problem solving is to understand the problem and the scope of the issue. A good way to do so is by identifying the key points of the problem and writing them down. This will help conduct research to find relevant resources and have discussions with peers or supervisors.
- **Acquire technical knowledge:** As a PhD student, one already has a chosen field of interest. In order to be a good problem solver, one must acquire all possible technical knowledge there is to gain in the said field of study.
- **Take every opportunity to solve problem:** Orienting one's mind to look at every problem as an opportunity to learn something new and improve their knowledge base. When one seeks out opportunities to solve problems, they learn something about the problem and themselves. This enables them to grow and hone their problem solving skills over time.

- **Practice makes a man perfect:** Whether it is a simple mathematical problem or everyday struggles, when one practices problem solving every day, they are able to reorient their minds to quickly enter problem solving mode when they are faced with one.
- **Learn from others:** One of the best ways to learn how to solve problems is by observing others. This technique will allow PhD students to view and understand the process of problem solving employed by others, which is often different or even unique. Observing others tackling their problems can help upgrade one's problem solving skills.
- **Focus on the solution, not the problem:** Students often get overwhelmed with problem to the extent that they are unable to think or act rationally. A key way to effectively solve problems is to focus on finding a solution than fretting about the problem at hand. This will also minimize the negative implications on one's mind like stress, anxiety, and frustration.
- **Develop logical and critical thinking:** Logical and critical thinking is an integral part of conducting any form

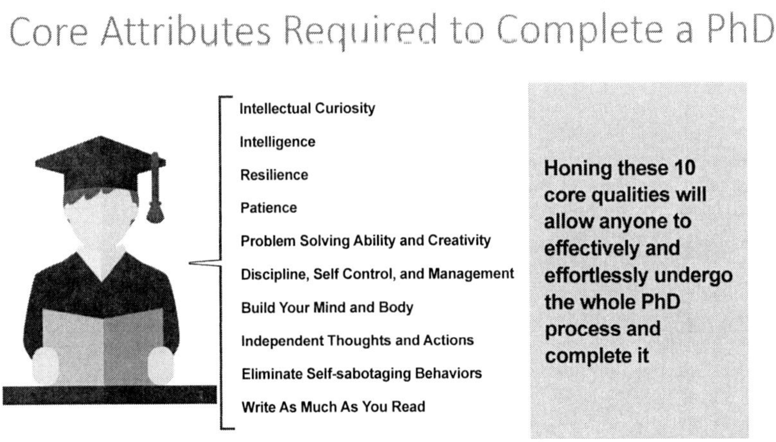

Figure 4: Core Attributes Required to Complete a PhD

of research. It is driven by facts, numbers and reasons, which come together in understanding and analysing the problem. Developing the ability to think analytically will significantly improve one's problem solving skills.

Problem solving skill is an important skill, which takes time and a focused effort to develop. Every PhD student will find this skill to be helpful in not only an academic sense but also in his or her everyday life. Therefore, mastering the art of problem solving will play a vital role in facilitating the successful completion of any PhD program.

6. Discipline, self-control, and time management

As a young PhD student, one of the greatest challenges faced is self-control. As youngsters, the desire to have a good social life is strong. One feels lured to enjoy the various leisure of life like watching movies, going to clubs, traveling, partying etc. A good mantra to follow when faced with a dilemma is that *everything is good and acceptable in moderation.*

While taking occasional breaks and changing up the pace is good for both mind and body, forming an extreme and extravagant social lifestyle can hamper the academic pursuits of PhD students. It is essential to train one's mind to not give into the temptations and indulge in social activities for months on end. There are many strategies on how to train your mind and override impulses.

- **Remove Temptations:** Our minds can sometimes play tricks on us making it difficult to resist temptations. Despite our best efforts, it can be challenging to control our impulses to indulge in various distracting temptations. The key here is to remove any and all temptations from the equation. By doing so you set yourself up for success and manage yourself better leading a disciplined lifestyle.

- **Prioritize your goals:** Success comes to those who are disciplined and make a conscious decision to prioritize their goals. Simple steps like making a to-do list every day to keep a track of everyday progress will help stay on course and instill a sense of control and discipline.
- **Target based rewards:** A great way to prevent distractions is by setting up a reward system where upon successfully completing a target you get a predefined reward. This way you stay motivated to complete the task with dedication and discipline.
- **Remember why:** Every time you feel distracted or urged to give into the temptations, remind yourself why you chose to do a PhD and would it mean to accomplish such a degree. Never forget why and where you started. This has often helped students refocus their energy towards their goals.
- **Choose your friends wisely:** Your social circle can impact your motivation and discipline. If you spend too much time interacting with people who are not committed to their academic goals, you may feel deterred from focusing on your goals as well. Instead, surround yourself with people and friends who will hold you accountable and encourage you, especially when things get tough.

Protecting yourself from distractions is hard but incorporating these simple tricks can ensure you stay disciplined and resist any and all temptations. Discipline and self-control are two traits leading the way to success.

7. Build your mind and body

Pursuing PhD is incredibly exciting time in one's life. You are surrounded by colleagues and peers who are working towards a similar goal. It is a time of tremendous hard work but it can also turn into a sedentary lifestyle where one spends countless hours reading, researching, and writing. To save time or stick to their schedules, students often turn to take out meals or even skip them. Falling prey to such unhealthy patterns negatively impacts the one's mental and physical health.

More often than not, focusing on one's wellbeing has never been the priority. They are too overwhelmed and preoccupied with their academic commitments that rarely do they find time to work out or engage in any form of exercise. What most don't realize is that tirelessly working may seem fruitful in the beginning but overworking can lead to exhaustion, sluggishness, mood swings which would result in poor performance and deteriorating health. A few small changes in the lifestyle can improve your productivity, boost your mood and keep you healthy. Here's how you can build your mind and body

- **Start small:** When one starts working out the temptation to go all in strong. However, take baby steps that are manageable and achievable. Build the habit of working out and then slowly expand as you go. This leads to consistency.
- **Customize it to your needs:** Choose a mode of workout that suits you best. If you don't like going to the gym and prefer running, then do that. Working out should not feel like a punishment rather be a rejuvenating experience. Figure out what you enjoy and it will be easy to stick with it.

- **Set a time for it:** Working out takes up time and allotting a set amount of time for it can help in planning your daily activities accordingly and get into the habit of working out. Be realistic of time you are willing to devote towards it and try to stay committed to it.
- **Little goes a long way:** You don't need to punch in three hours of exercise, seven days a week to stay healthy. All you need to do is take some time out to train your body enough to deal with the physical and mental stress that comes with an intensive PhD program.
- **Meditation works:** Many PhD students struggle with managing the stress and anxiety. One of the proven methods to deal with them is by practicing mindfulness. Meditation or simple moments of guided mindfulness can significantly reduce stress and anxiety. Paying attention to one's mental health has been proven to be helpful in PhD journey.

PhD process can be physically and emotionally draining. Students are expected to do work long nights and long days or wake up early to work on their research. In some cases, the research takes the students on a physically taxing journey or hours of physical activity. This takes a toll on their health and wellbeing. Therefore, students must build themselves up for an extensive and demand program like PhD.

8. Be independent in your thoughts/actions

The ability to work and think independently is one of the basic prerequisites for any research degree program, more so for PhD. One must be prepared to work alone and micromanage themselves easily. It requires one to develop qualities like confidence, initiative, and the sense of responsibility.

They should demonstrate the ability to work with minimal supervision. However, that doesn't mean that there shouldn't be any discussion with the supervisor. The idea is to grow independently and limit these discussions to important and essential aspects of study. Independence of thought is an essential attribute that one needs to hone as their PhD study progresses. Ideally, a student should be able to work alone, ask questions, and pursue their own lines of thought to truly excel in research. Students who take ownership of their projects, are proactive and are keen on working independently are easily able to successfully complete their PhD.

People who successfully complete PhD are disciplined. They are capable of working autonomously, sticking to self-imposed deadlines, and focusing on the big picture. They throw themselves into the study of best writing practices, keep a strict schedule, form writing accountability groups, and work out parts of the thesis during the process. They should be able to grow and become the best version of themselves. Someone, who is able to create a workflow for the course of their study, stay on track, and be self-motivating without being dependent on any external force.

Lack of independence is often accompanied by lack of confidence and initiative, dependence on others for everything, fear of failure, and demonstrate various self-sabotaging attributes that affect their performance and chances of completing their degree. One must possess following attributes to work independently:

- ✓ Ability to come up with new and unique ideas
- ✓ Create and follow a routine
- ✓ Fix problems by oneself

- ✓ Take responsibility and accountability for various aspect of research
- ✓ Make mistakes and rectify them

The ability to research, think, and work logically and independently is one of the vital skills required in PhD. The ability to take ownership of one's research with minimal supervision will help tremendously in accomplishing a PhD degree.

9. Eliminate self-sabotaging behaviors

Completing a PhD degree is one of the most challenging yet fulfilling academic and life experiences. Besides intellect, it is a test of one's grit and determination. While there are many challenges on your paths, the most dangerous and difficult hurdle to overcome is one's own self, more precisely self-sabotaging behavior.

What are self-sabotaging behaviors? They are actions and mindsets that deliberately prevent one from achieving and accomplishing their goals. PhD students are particularly susceptible to self-sabotaging behavioral traits like perfectionism, procrastination and imposter syndrome. Many students are unaware of existence of such traits within them and some are unable to overcome them.

Here are some common ways that PhD students sabotage their PhD studies and techniques to prevent them:

- **Procrastination:** The number one behavioral challenge most people face, whether they are PhD student or from any other profession, is procrastination. It is the tendency to avoid doing anything that one needs to do. There is always something you put off something for a later time because you are distracted or feeling lazy or you fell in the rabbit hole of Internet! We all have been there. More often than we would like to admit. But that doesn't mean that we must let it become a habit. There are very simple ways to break the chain and get work done. Do not procrastinate the following:

- ✓ Just start working
- ✓ Have a designated workspace
- ✓ Turn off all kinds of distractions
- ✓ Breakdown work into smaller tasks
- ✓ Create achievable timetables and stick to them
- ✓ Overcome your fear of failure.
- ✓ Develop a positive mindset

- **Perfectionism:** A common obstacle hampering productivity and performance of doctoral students is perfectionism. It is nothing but setting highly unrealistic and impossible standards or expectations that prevents them from putting their best foot forward. For instance, some students have high standard for writing their thesis or the timeline for writing it. While others assume that people around them have set high standards for their work and that it must be met in order to avoid disapproval. This projection of supposed expectation imposed by others restricts the perfectionist. They then struggle to keep up, stay motivated and productive when the focus is on performing well or as per expectations. This pressure diminishes their confidence, interest and desire to do accomplish anything. There is fear of being viewed as flawed or inadequate forces one to create an illusion of perfection. Although this may offer a sense of control and quell the uncertainty, self-doubt and anxiety, it pushes you further away from reality. Tips for perfectionism:

  - ✓ Identify, acknowledge and let go of high and unrealistic standards.

- ✓ Replace excessive expectations with reasonable alternatives.
- ✓ Practice patience and trust the process.
- ✓ Keep working towards your goal without overthinking.
- ✓ Take feedback as positively and integrate the inputs.
- ✓ Draw a line and accept that your work is “enough”

- **Imposter syndrome:** The biggest challenge faced by most doctoral students is the feeling of being a fraud, sometimes referred to as ‘Imposter Syndrome’. It is an overwhelming feeling that in time someone will “find out” you are “fake”. Students facing this usually convince themselves that it is true and that they are unworthy and stupid. They truly believe that they’d get caught and be humiliated. Thoughts like “Everyone will realise that you’re too stupid to do a PhD”, “What on earth were you thinking?” and “How did you even believe that you could write a thesis?” take over. While these are very unsettling feelings but they are perfectly normal and nearly every PhD student experiences them at some point or the other. However, not many are willing to admit it. The nature of PhD is such that every time you begin to make some progress, you’re challenged by new ideas or data. The closer you get to success or completion, the more insecure you begin to feel. What helps to tackle this is by not attaching any grand value to it. Accept that it is simply a part of the process. Don’t let the feeling dominate your thought process. Talk to someone if the feeling takes over everything and restricts you.
- **Overcommitting:** Students, including doctoral candidates, feel that the more workload they take, the better their chances are in succeeding in life. In addition

to all the course work, PhD students try to say "yes" to every opportunity that comes their way in the hopes to establish themselves in the academic world. However, this does not always turn out well. They take up more work than they can handle which often results in either poor quality of work and builds a bad reputation. Taking on more than one can handle or overcommitting can cause more damage than good. The ability to say "no" and respectfully declining opportunities is perhaps one of the greatest traits one can possess. Overpromising, overextending, overestimating and overdoing does not allow one to live a balanced life, care for themselves or cultivate a positive and healthy professional identity. Tips to avoid overcommitting:

- ✓ Before making a commitment, take a moment to check your schedule and contemplate whether you will be able to include this project and do justice to it without compromising on other activities and commitments.
- ✓ Prioritize your schedule based on various parameters suitable to you. Be realistic in your approach.
- ✓ Avoid any last minute opportunity no matter how appealing they may seem. Again, be realistic.
- ✓ Never schedule anything by replacing your "me time". You need time to rest and reset.
- ✓ Learn to say "no" and mean it no matter how hard it seems. Only you know the extent of your workload so it is important that you learn to set limits.

Self-sabotaging tendencies are deeply rooted in counterproductive mindsets like procrastination, perfectionism, negativity, disorganization, and imposter syndrome. As doctoral student, one must learn to recognize these negative and avoiding behaviors as they holds us back from progressing and succeeding.

10. Write as much as you read

PhD, to put it simply, is a reading and writing exercise. You read something and you write something – preferably, one page per day. This can be achieved by setting aside at least 30 minutes daily to write down something related to your thesis, which could be a note from what you are reading, a summary of ideas or simply thoughts that occurred to you related to your work.

Writing is a cathartic exercise and provides an aesthetic experience. It helps you think and gather your thoughts that formulates into an idea. Writing crystallizes your thoughts. It gives clarity and lucidity to your ideas. As a researcher, you have a wide range of ideas but they never appear to be good enough. This is usually because you haven't written them into existence. Once you write them down, you give them a new dimension where there is scope for further exploration. Don't worry about drafting a perfect piece of scholarly article at the first go. Start by outlining your main ideas and elucidating with examples or explanations. As you write, there will be free flow of ideas and you will be a step closer to writing an insightful scholarly paper yourself. It is important that you don't wait for the perfect paper to be written but write it instead!

As a graduate student, the biggest challenge is writing your dissertation. To write a good dissertation, it is not only important to research and read but also important to write. Writing about the topic makes you think of it in a different light, which wouldn't have been possible just talking about it. Once you have made up your mind about a topic, my advise is to get into the habit of writing every day. It will enable you to become a prolific writer with well-organized and constructive ideas. It will simplify the dissertation writing process into a less stressful and rather enjoyable one.

It is imperative for any graduate researcher to write every day because writing is thinking. Quite often, graduate students procrastinate and wait for their 'Eureka' moment when ideas would flow into paper. But, that's never the case. Any good piece of writing is a product of several drafts. It is absolutely crucial to keep a written record of your ideas and thoughts because anything that is written can be improved and developed. If you follow a writing routine, you will have the opportunity to enhance it and make it better. So instead of simply thinking about it or discussing with your fellow researchers, get in the habit of writing. You will be surprised to see how this habit will help you in writing your final dissertation or scholarly article.

A typical PhD thesis is about 220+ pages, approximately 80,000 to 100,000 words including preliminary pages, references and appendices. So, if you write 1 page per day, you can get thesis done in one year. Here's how: there are about 220 workdays in a year (Monday - Friday) and 52 weeks in a year. If you manage to write 1 page per day 5 pages per week, you will have at least 260 pages worth work done! Now, it does sound easy on paper but can be difficult to put in action.

To start off, I recommend adopting the '10-10-10 principle'. A simple principle is extremely helpful and effective.

This is a three-step process:

Step one: When you have decided on the topic, shortlist 10 different journals relevant to your study. Make use of the Internet and university library to search for journals relevant to your topic.

Step two: Pick out 10 articles that you believe are relevant to your area of interest. Read the title and abstract in order to judge their relevance. Avoid three years old articles (because they are obviously outdated).

Step three: Spend some quality time reading and understanding these articles. Once you finish reading, write about them. This should be no longer than one page.

This brief write-up is called an Annotated Bibliography. This exercise helps you judge the relevance, accuracy, and quality of the research articles and of your study. I suggest the following structure to make the most of this exercise:

1. Begin with the title on top of the page and make sure you give the APA citation of the title.
2. In a sentence explain the problem--that will be your problem statement. You can write about it in three sentences.
3. State primary sources that the article is based on. Write at least three to four sentences.
4. In at least three sentences, explain the methodology used in the study.
5. Describe the finding of the study briefly. You should write about three to four sentences about the results.
6. Finally, write about the prospective research ideas discussed in the study. Mention further research ideas in about four sentences.
7. The purpose of this activity is to help you understand the subject matter better and become aware of various studies going on in the field. This is an extremely fruitful activity, as by the end of it, you are sure to find your exact research topic.

This exercise is a guideline for every researcher, especially novice researchers. This is how you arrive at a good problem statement as well as get into the habit of writing a page a day.

Therefore, the first step in your journey of research should always be the 10-10-10 principle.

10-10-10 Principle

10/10/10

1)- Shorlist 10 journals relevant to your study

2)- Pick 10 articles that are relevant to you

3)- Read & understand those 10 articles, then start writing about it

PhD Topic Selection

The very rudimentary step to the research process involves the selection of a topic and a research area. Choosing an ultimate doctoral dissertation topic is perhaps one of the most important and rather daunting decision that any student will make during graduate school. It is the single biggest hurdle to overcome in order to complete PhD. Once a good topic is decided and finalized, 30% of the thesis is done. Choosing a research topic is regarded as an integral part of the PhD that significantly contributes to the successful completion of the program. It is important to choose a topic in an area where one has built expertise and experience, and also, where one has great passion and interest in as this will sustain the student through the process leading to completion. The chosen topic should not be too broad such that completion becomes impossible and should not be too narrow such that it restricts scholar's original contribution. Adhikari (2020) stated that it is important that the topic has scientific, social or practical relevance, makes an original contribution to the field, and is useful to other researchers, practitioners and policy makers. Choosing a topic, which eventually proves to be vague, undoable and flawed, stresses out the student and leads to dropout. Whereas, choosing a good topic guarantees timely PhD completion, high impact research, quick postdoctoral placement, as well as accelerated career path.

Most students would have already spent their early graduate school years looking for potential topics before finally selecting one for their thesis. It is definitely the most critical decision and a lot depends on the doctoral dissertation research topic they select. Even with the growth of information technology, many graduate students worldwide view the research topic selection process to be quite stressful and time-consuming. They are afraid of finding and eventually selecting a topic completely on their own. But this is no longer a major problem for a student with well-developed skills in information searching. However, with the Internet being the main domain of information for students there is a potential risk of being overwhelmed by information and coming across erroneous or misleading information. Therefore, students must find out what professors and scholars have commented on a topic, perhaps this topic is exciting enough to capture their attention for further research in the next several years. Many researchers argue that there is a strong tie between PhD research and supervisor's own research. This means that most students are not independent in choosing their own topics in which they feel comfortable and this may result in non-completion. If a student is able to choose his own topic, this automatically means that he may also be able to write the thesis and accomplish on time. He will need to ask and answer some questions while selecting and evaluating a research topic.

Questions to ask Yourself Before Choosing a PhD Research Topic

1. What research area am I interested in or passionate about?
2. What problem do I want to solve?
3. Who cares about this problem?
4. What have others done to solve this problem?
5. How much information do I have about the topic through existing knowledge and prior reading?
6. Are there sufficient/relevant data available for the topic?
7. Would I have easy access to gathering the information needed for the research?
8. Are there new dimensions in the research area that will contribute to existing knowledge?
9. How much effort, time, and cost will be needed for data collection?
10. Is the research scope realistic and can be completed within 3-5 years?

Three things to consider when choosing a topic:

1. Pick a topic that will help you professionally.
2. Pick a topic you will be happy to talk about at any given time.
3. Pick a topic that will be useful to people for years to come.

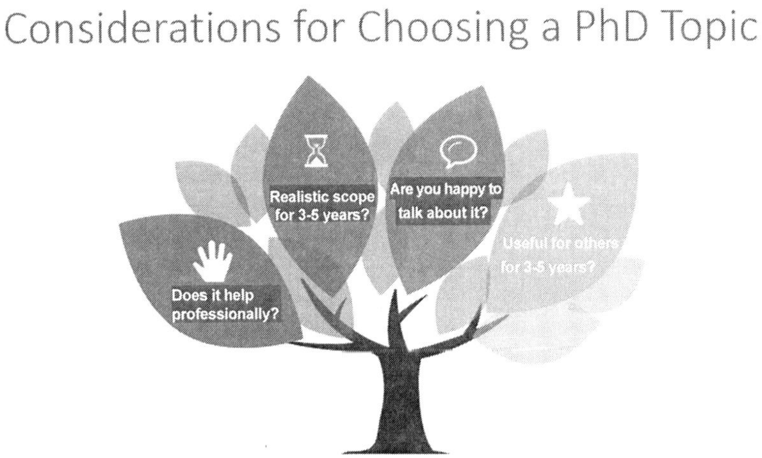

Figure 5: Considerations for Choosing a PhD Topic

Common Mistakes to Avoid While Choosing a Topic

1. Being fixated and excited about a particular topic without being open to review, criticism and suggestions.
2. Choosing an area of research where data collection is rigorous and almost impossible.
3. Choosing a topic with a broad scope that is impossible to cover.
4. Getting easily swayed by a new found research area or other people's view point.
5. Underestimation of scope, cost, time, and effort required.

❐

Chapter 5
A Framework for Selecting a Topic and Continuing the Thesis

It is an already established fact that selecting a PhD thesis topic is a crucial part of completing PhD. For the topic selection framework, I'm introducing the 10 – 10 – 10 approach where;

- The first 10 means 10 journals.
- The second 10 means 10 articles.
- The third 10 means 10 annotated bibliographies or summary of each article (one page).

Step 1: Develop a potential topic (keywords) in your area of research interest: Keywords helps to identify the topic's main concept and it has a huge impact on the search for articles related to the topic. In order to identify appropriate keywords, you have to decide on a research question or phrase the topic in form of a question you would like to answer.

Look at an example;

- Proposed title in form of a question.

  "Does Social Networking Sites Prevent Students from Learning"
- Key concepts/keywords

Social Networking Sites	**Students**
Facebook	Learners
Twitter	High School Students

Instagram Undergraduates
Snapchat Postgraduates
WhatsApp
Tiktok

With this, a potential topic in form of a research question has been developed and keywords have been identified with more background information. The topic can then be refined based on the additional information.

Step 2: Find top 10 reputable journals in your area of research: The search for relevant journals can be a daunting task for new and even experienced researchers. This is attributed to the rise in the number of open and close access journals, preprint repositories, and varying databases. According to Dixon et al., (2010), finding journal titles and journal articles are two of the toughest tasks on academic library web pages and this challenge includes choosing the best tools and using terms that make sense. To aid the search for journals in terms of quality, publication details, journal metrics, web of science coverage, and peer review characteristics, the following tools can help you to confidently find, access, and assess journals.

1. Journal Citation Reports (JCR)
2. Master Journal List (MJL)
3. Web of Science
4. Google Scholar

What to Look Out for When Searching for Quality Journals

1. Ensure that the journals are indexed in Google scholar, Scopus, web of science, PubMed, Citeseer, JSTOR or CINAHL.

2. The journal has a website that has been in existence for a reasonable number of years with relevant information on authors and readers.
3. The editorial board consists of professors, lecturers, and researchers from accredited academic and research institutions.
4. There is an online version of the journal.
5. Manuscripts are peer reviewed for publication.
6. Digital Object Identifiers (DOI) are assigned to all articles.

Step 3: Within the 10 journals, pick one article from each journal based on your interest in the title of the article. Ensure that the articles were published within the last three years so as to base your research on current information. Avoid referencing old articles as much as you can as they may have become obsolete and the ideas may not be appropriate to use in solving current issues. For example;

Journal Name: Journal of Education and Practice. ISSN: 2222-1735 (Paper), ISSN: 2222-288X (Online). Vol. 9 No. 20, 2018.

Article: Iroegbu, E. E. (2018). Social networking sites usage and the negative influence on students' academic achievement in high school. *Journal of Education and Practice, 9*(20), 82-92.

From the topic sample given in step one, the article chosen in step 3 is closely related which indicates that the right article that will aid the current research has been chosen.

Step 4: Read only the abstract, introduction, subheadings, and conclusion: For all the 10 articles chosen from each journal, reading these sections of the article enables you to quickly determine if the article has important details that support your main ideas. It also gives you the opportunity to identify the key points that will be relevant to your research.

Abstract: This carries information about the purpose of research, sample size, methodology used, significant results, implication and recommendation. It gives a summary of the research that was conducted and an overview of what to expect from the article.

Headings and Subheadings: This gives you a quick idea of the content of the article and what each section is talking about.

Introduction and Conclusion: These sections outline what the author sets out to achieve and the outcome of the exercise.

Step 5: Write a summary of one page per chosen article: Writing research summary also called annotated bibliography entails going through each part of the article and extracting the essential points leaving out anything that can be considered as supplementary detail. Each article should be summarized under the following headings;

Title: The title of the article

Citation: This indicates how the article should eventually be referenced if the article was cited. Information under this heading includes author name and initials, date of publication, article title, title of publication, volume, issue, page numbers, and either a DOI or URL.

Introduction: This part outlines the purpose of the study, problem statement, theories used, research question, and hypothesis formulated.

Methods: This part states what type of research was done and how relevant data was collected and analyzed.

Results: What were the major findings and was the hypothesis formulated supported.

Conclusion: Authors' opinion about the outcome, limitations, implications, recommendations, and future research opportunities.

Justification: This part clearly states how this article is related and relevant to your research.

Step 6: At the end of this exercise, you have completed the 10 – 10 – 10 approach comprising;

- 10 Journals
- 10 Articles
- 10 pages of write-up

Step 7: Look through the future research direction section of the ten summarized articles. This section of a research article clearly states a possible futuristic research path and why the path may be relevant for current studies. From this section, you will be able to generate the following for your thesis;

- **Problem Statement:** Problem statement is an integral part the research that states what problem a particular study intends to solve and why the study matters. Grant and Osanloo (2019) declared that problem statement establishes an interaction by two or more factors that produce a dilemma or quandary that can cause further examining and also defines the root problem as well as other variables and constructs inherent to the problem. Most times, problem statement is usually confused with thesis statement and research question. Although they are all related, they mean entirely different things and they play specific roles in a study. See their respective meanings;
- *Problem Statement*: This is the problem the study is set out to tackle.
- *Research Question*: This is usually centered around the research problem and its aim is to guide your research in a specific direction.
- *Thesis Statement*: This is the answer to your research question and the ultimate argument of your thesis.

Problem Statement Template to Follow When Defining a Research Problem

- *1st Sentence*: Give a background information of your research problem in terms of what we already know about the problem.
- *2nd Sentence*: Clearly state what the research problem is.
- *3rd Sentence*: Describe how important the problem is and why it needs to be solved.
- **Purpose of the Study:** The purpose of the study discusses the comparisons that will be made in the study, defines research objectives, and introduces research questions and hypotheses. The three most common purposes are exploration, description, and explanation. Quantitative research purpose statements focus on correlating measurable variables whilc qualitative research purpose explores a specific idea.
- **Research Question:** Research questions presents an opportunity to learn about a phenomenon or problem in a refined way. It also indicates the specific angle of a phenomenon a researcher wishes to examine. Mattick et al., (2018) stated that a research question is a question that a research project sets to answer and good research questions seek to improve knowledge on an important topic.

The Essence of Future Research Suggestions

- To build upon the research findings especially the unexpected findings and areas where the current study could not cover.
- To propose future research areas which will address the limitations encountered in the course of the study.

- To see if similar results could be generated if the same study is conducted in a different location, culture, context or settings.

Step 8: Review of related literature: Literature review is a part of the research process where related studies are described, discussed and analyzed. It helps to determine what is known and unknown about a research topic and subsequently leads to the generation of research question and hypothesis for a new study. Fink (2014) stated that a literature review surveys books, scholarly articles and any other sources relevant to a particular issue, area of research, or theory, and by so doing, provides a description, summary, and critical evaluation of these works in relation to the research problem being investigated. Literature review entails summarizing the best methods (methodology) used to solve similar problems. It has an organizational pattern where it combines summary and synthesis, where summary is a recap of relevant information extracted from an article while synthesis entails reshuffling or re-organizing the information. Literature reviews are designed to provide an overview of sources you have explored while researching a particular topic and to demonstrate to your readers how your research fits within a larger field of study (Fink, 2014).

Purpose of Literature Review

- It acts as a stepping stone to develop a new argument.
- It creates a handy guide to a particular research topic.
- It keeps you up to date with what is current in a particular area of research.
- It describes the relationship of each source to the others you have selected.

- It emphasizes the credibility of the writer in a particular field of study.
- It points the way forward for further research.

Ways to Organize Your Literature Review

Chronology of Events: It entails writing the review according to when the materials were published by tracing the development of the topic over time. This method is appropriate if a clear path of research has been identified and whose trend follows a clear order of development.

Thematic: Here, literature is organized into subsections that address different aspects of the research.

Theoretical: Various theories, models or key concepts are discussed and combined to create a framework for your research.

Methodological: If the sources of literature reviews are drawn from different fields of study that uses varying research methods, the results could be compared in the following ways:

- Qualitative versus quantitative study.
- Empirical approach versus theoretical scholarship.
- Reviews could also be grouped into cultural, historical, and sociological.

Three Basic Elements of Literature Review

1. *Introduction*

- Introduce the topic and area of research.
- Describe the overall trend based on what has been published about the topic in terms of gaps in research, methodology, theoretical conflicts, evidence, problem or new perspective.

- State your reason for the literature review.
- Explain the criteria to be used in comparing and analyzing the literature review.
- State how the review will be organized.

2. *Body*

- Summarize individual studies with as much or as little details as needed and organize them either chronologically, thematically, theoretically or methodologically.

3. *Conclusion*

- State the major contribution of each reviewed article to the body of knowledge.
- Point out major gaps and methodological flaws.
- State issues pertinent to future studies.

The following issues should be considered when writing literature review:

- Be selective of the information you choose to highlight in your review by ensuring that the chosen information relates to your problem statement.
- Do not base your review on assumptions, any interpretation of sources must be well cited.
- Use short quote only when the author's statement cannot be paraphrased, otherwise, avoid the use of quotes.
- Restate the significance of the study and how it relates to your work.
- Keep the author's authentic voice and message when paraphrasing and cite appropriately.
- Keep your own voice by starting and ending the paragraph with your own ideas and words.

Literature Research is not about throwing some text paragraphs in thesis, but it is a story telling skill about problem statement. Every paragraph in literature review means something to problem statement. At the end of literature review, you have to summarize what is known about the problem and what is unknown in the body of knowledge; identify how the literature content in the individual articles of your literature relates to the concepts you discovered; and show how your topic of problem statement will solve the unknown portion of the body of knowledge. It is important that you develop and present your own organization and understanding of the literature. By this, you will end up with a review that is organized by the concepts and relationship you found and developed based on your reading and thinking. Your literature will not only cover what is known about your problem statement, but will include your own thoughts and ideas.

Step 9: Selecting research methodology: There has been a heightened need to use appropriate research methodologies and methods to answer research questions, and by this, there is no right or wrong approach in selecting methodology. The most important aspect of choosing any methodology is your ability to justify and convince readers as to why that particular methodology was chosen and how it suits your perspective. Research methodology refers to the research approach, particularly the various types of activities to systematically address the research challenge, which is based on assumptions and justification of the choices made (Wohlin & Runeson, 2021). Methodology should contain relevant information to enable the reader understand what was done and how it was done.

Research methods and research methodology have often been used interchangeably and confused, but they mean two different things. Research methodology is the primary principle that will guide your research and it determines what research method to use while research methods are the tools you use to gather your data (Dawson, 2019). To further clarify the difference, Surbhi (2018) referred to research method as the technique which can be adopted to explore the nature of the world around us while research methodology is the foundation which helps us to understand the determinants influencing the effectiveness of the methods applied. Surbhi went further to develop a comparison chart as shown below:

Basis of Comparison	**Research Method**	**Research Methodology**
Meaning	Research method implies the methods employed by the researcher to conduct research.	Research methodology signifies way to efficiently solving research problems.
What is it?	Behavior and instrument used in the selection and construction of the research technique.	Science of understanding how research is performed methodically.
Encompasses	Carrying out experiment, test, surveys and so on.	Study different techniques which can be utilized in the performance of experiment, test, surveys etc.
Comprise of	Different investigation techniques.	Entire strategy towards achievement of objective.
Objective	To discover solution to research problem.	To apply correct procedures so as to determine solutions.

Source: Surbhi (2018).

Before choosing a research methodology, it is important to have a good understanding of the three major types of research since they all use different methodological approach.

1. **Qualitative Research:** This form of research focuses on concepts, explorations, descriptions, values, beliefs,

intangibles, and words. It is mostly based on personal opinions; uses an inductive and subjective approach; draws on small sample sizes; uses content and thematic analysis techniques; and it is not number-based. Qualitative research methodologies examine the behaviors, opinions, and experiences of individuals through methods of examination (Dawson, 2019). The method of collecting data for qualitative research includes focus groups, observation, open-ended questionnaires, semi-structured interviews, theoretical analysis and unstructured interviews. Qualitative research is of different types such as ethnographic, phenomenological, grounded theory, historical, case study, and action research. Example of an area of study that would need a qualitative study would be that of supervisory styles adopted by PhD supervisors where data is mostly gathered through interviews.

2. **Quantitative Research:** This form of research uses statistics and numbers to measure the nature of relationship, determine differences between variables, test and confirm hypotheses, as well as verify theories. Close-ended questionnaires/surveys, structured interviews, and laboratory experiments are often used to collect number-based data from large sample sizes. Quantitative research uses a deductive and objective approach, as well as statistical data analysis techniques. According to Labaree (2020), there are three parts that make up a quantitative research methodology:

- Sample population
- How you will collect your data (this is the research method)
- How you will analyze your data

3. **Mixed Methods:** This is a combination of both qualitative and quantitative research where a conceptual

framework is developed using qualitative research and the framework is empirically tested using quantitative methods. Close-ended and open-ended questionnaires are used to collect data for mixed methods research. An example of a mixed method is a study in which statistical data is gathered through questionnaires, backed up by interviewing few people from the research sample size.

Other types of research methodologies are descriptive, analytical, applied, fundamental, exploratory, and conclusive research.

The choice of an appropriate research method depends largely on research objectives. According to Dawson (2019), there are several questions to ask yourself when determining the best research method for your project:

- Are you good with numbers and mathematics?
- Would you be interested in conducting interviews with human subjects?
- Would you enjoy creating a questionnaire for participants to complete?
- Do you prefer written communication or face-to-face interaction?
- What skills or experiences do you have that might help you with your research? Do you have any experiences from past research projects that can help with this one?
- How much time do you have to complete the research? Some methods take longer to collect data than others.
- What is your budget? Do you have adequate funding to conduct the research in the method you want?
- How much data do you need? Some research topics need only small amount of data while others may need significantly larger amounts.

- What is the purpose of your research? This can provide a good indicator as to what research method will be most appropriate.

Steps to Follow While Choosing Appropriate Methodology

First: Have a clear understanding of what you want to study by determining your research objectives, questions, and variables. If it is exploratory, adopt a qualitative approach, if it is confirming a hypothesis, adopt a quantitative approach, and if it combines a mix of both, then use the mixed methods approach.

Second: Evaluate the methodologies commonly and effectively used in the related literatures reviewed and see if it fits into the context of your research.

Third: Check the constraints and practicalities involved which are in form of easy access to data, cost, equipment and software needed, as well as your experience and expertise.

Fourth: Review the chosen methodology and make a note of all the activities involved.

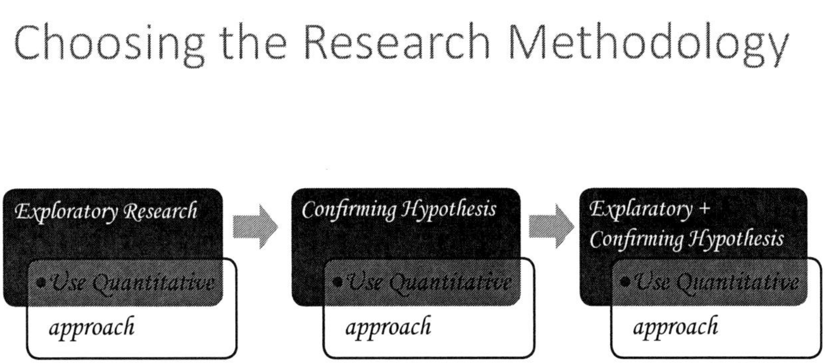

Justifying Your Choice of Methodology

One of the most difficult aspect of putting together a quantitative methodology is to find the foundational references that justifies your choice of a particular research methodology. Methodology is all about justifying chosen approach to solve the problem statement. You justify with at least 3 citations from the literature. There is no right or wrong in methodology. Everything in methodology is about justification. You should be able to convince and make justifications to readers why you chose that particular research method and how it suits your objective. Always relate your choice of research method to the main purpose of your thesis. A well written methodology section must justify rationale for chosen research methods and procedures. While justifying your choice of methodology, cite all the sources you used to determine your choice of methodology. This reinforces the validity of your research.

Justification could be about methodology, chosen sample size, chosen data analysis techniques, chosen assumptions etc. Take for instance, in choosing a qualitative design, the following text could be used to support your choice of design based on the purpose. In ethnographic research design, the researcher aims to study the participants' culture and society through investigating their beliefs and values that shape their behaviors in a specific society (Merriam, 2009). In case study design, researcher aims to "investigate a contemporary phenomenon in depth and within its real-life context" (Yin, 2009, p. 18). In grounded theory design, the researcher aims to develop a theory that grounded in the field-based data that collected from the study participants and hold their perspectives regarding the phenomenon under study (Merriam, 2009).

To justify your choice of sampling technique, the following texts could be used to support your choice. The sample types are varied based on the research's approach. In quantitative research approach, a probability sampling is needed as the researcher aims to generalize the results to a bigger population (Merriam, 2009). In qualitative research approach, however, non-probability sampling is needed as the researcher aims to understand the phenomenon under study not to generalize the research results (Merriam, 2009). The purposeful sample concerns with the quality over quantity as purposeful sample of two participants might collect rich data for a qualitative study such as narrative research (Creswell, 2013). Furthermore, Creswell (2013) asserted that the size of the selected sample is based on the type of the qualitative study and suggested a sample of 3 to 10 participants to collect data for phenomenological studies and 20 to 30 participants to collect enough data for grounded theory.

Step 10: Results section: The results section is where the authors inform the readers about the findings from the statistical analysis of the data collected to operationalize the study hypothesis, optimally adding novel information to the collective knowledge on the subject matter (Snyder et al., 2019). The results section is where you report the findings of your study based upon the methodology you applied to gather information and should also state the findings of the research arranged in a logical sequence without bias or interpretation (Annesley, 2010a). Kroemer (2020) gave the following tips:

Tips to Write the Result Section

- Direct the reader to the research data and explain the meaning of the data.
- Avoid using a repetitive sentence structure to explain a new set of data.
- Write and highlight the important findings in your results.

- Use the same order as the subheadings of the methods section.
- Match the results with the research questions from the introduction. Your results should answer your research questions.
- Make sure there is no mismatch of the table number in text and in figure/tables.
- Only present data that support the significance of your study. You can provide additional data in tables and figures as supplementary material.

One way to organize the structure of the discussion section is by dividing into three parts (Ghasemi, 2019):

1. **The Beginning Part:** The first sentence of the first paragraph should state the importance and the new findings of your research. The first paragraph may also include answers to your research questions mentioned in the introduction section.
2. **The Middle Part:** The middle should contain the interpretations of the results to defend your answers, the strength of the study, and an update on literature review that validates your findings.
3. **The End Part:** The end concludes the study and the significance of your research.

Step 11: Discussion section: This section usually comes after the methods and results section, and before the conclusion. Discussion section can be a bit tasking as it entails evaluating the research that was conducted in relation to the theoretical body of knowledge on the topic. It also shows how relevant the findings are to professionals in the field being examined. The section is strictly based on specific stated objectives and research questions that were answered. Annesley (2010b) stated that the discussion will always connect to the introduction by way of the research questions or hypotheses you posed and the literature you reviewed, but the discussion does not simply repeat or rearrange the first parts of your paper; the discussion clearly explains how your study advanced the reader's understanding of the research problem from where you left them at the end of your review of prior research.

Information to Include in the Discussion Section

1. For each hypothesis formulated, clearly state the major findings of the study.
2. Interpret the findings.
3. Compare and indicate other researches with similar findings.
4. Explain any unexpected or inconclusive results.
5. Highlight how relevant your result is to those of from previous studies.

What to Leave out of the Discussion Section

- New reports that were not reported in the results section.
- Assumptions that are not supported by data.
- Don't discredit your research by elevating weaknesses and failures, rather, use the limitations to strengthen the credibility of your research.

Step 12: Conclusion: Conclusion is a short summary of what the research is all about. Andrade (2011) stated that conclusion should contain the most important take-home message of the study, additional findings of importance and the perspective expressed in a few precisely worded sentences. In research articles, the conclusion section is usually a combination of study limitations, recommendations and future research directions, but in thesis or dissertations, these sections are separately written. The conclusion section should;

- Restate the research questions and hypotheses that were answered and formulated.
- Restate major findings.
- Provide a synthesis of arguments presented in the study to show how they all come together to address the research objectives and questions.
- State its contribution to existing knowledge.

❐

Chapter 6

Further Research Suggestions

- There is a need for research on thorough identification of characteristics exhibited by PhD students who are at risk of dropout as this will enhance doctoral education practices.
- A study that critically analyses the advantages of virtual vs. traditional PhD should be conducted as this will encourage more online users since the traditional PhD is already well-known and widely accepted. This would have come in handy in the wake of Covid 19.
- A study that clearly defines variations in funding and how funding can be effectively managed to ensure completion of PhD is needed.
- There is a need for future research that is strictly focused on identifying and interviewing students who took longer time in completing their PhD, those who are in the later years of the program, and those who eventually dropped out. This purposive sampling will provide vital information needed to curb the high attrition rate.
- Research highlighting varying supervisory styles that will ensure completion should be carried out as this will ensure that supervisors do not resort to one style that fits all.

❐

Chapter 7

More Strategies for Ph.D Completion by Prof. Hamid H. Kazeroony

Writing a dissertation is simply an exercise in conducting scientific empirical research, observing ethical rules when conducting it while contributing meaningfully the body of knowledge. However, each doctoral researcher has time and financial constraint. Therefore, limiting the objectives of a dissertation would allow the researcher to complete the study in a timely fashion and financial resources. In this chapter we provide 10 strategies to (a) understand the organizational structure of a dissertation in simple terms, (b) simplify the process, and (c) remain on task and complete it successfully.

Writing a dissertation is a scaffolding process. First, we must review the peer-reviewed literature to find the gap. Once the gap is determined, then the problem statement is formulated. The purpose statement can be written based on the problem statement, outlining the research design. The wording in the problem statement and the purpose would lead us to a compelling research question. Once the gap, the problem, the purpose, and the research question have been stated, alignment between parts should be examined, ensuring all aspects are moving in the same direction. Then, we are in a position to address the intended population of the study, assumptions, scope, limitations, and delimitations, addressing the findings and maintaining positivity in light of various life obstacles as one attempt to complete the Ph.D. dissertation.

The Stepping-Stones for Ph.D. Completion

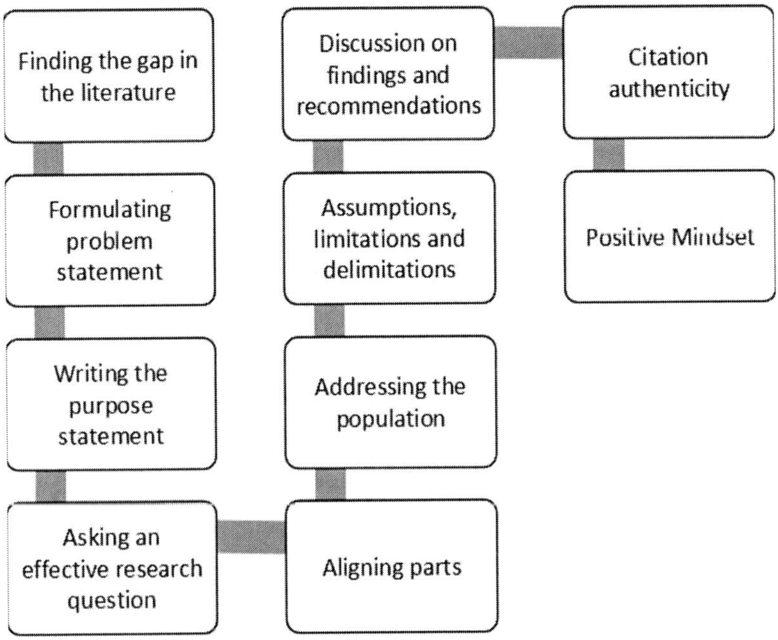

Figure 6: Top Ten Strategies for Ph.D. Completion by Prof. Hamid H. Kazeroony

Strategy 1: Finding the gap in the literature

Unlike a Doctor of Business Administration (DBA) project, the Ph.D. problem is rooted in peer-reviewed literature. A gap is a current issue in the peer-reviewed literature (Creswell, 1994) that requires addressing. A gap allows us to build on the existing body of knowledge to expand, deepen, or broaden what has already been known in a discipline, a particular domain of inquiry, and a paradigm (Kazeroony & Du Plessis, 2021).

Let us assume we are attempting to write a Ph.D. dissertation in History—a discipline. Let us further take that we are interested in the Russian Tzars—a domain of inquiry. Let us further assume that we are interested in examining the topic in a particular paradigm—worldview. Establishing the boundaries of the topic we want to address in a dissertation allows us to position the search when examining the peer-review literature correctly. The approach forces us to remain within the discipline that we intend to earn the Ph.D. degree, developing unique expertise in the domain of inquiry within a particular paradigm. In our history example, our Ph.D. degree would be in History, specializing in Russian Tzars, based on a paradigm that we adopt. The adaptation of this approach would allow us to proceed with finding an appropriate gap in the literature.

To find a gap in the literature, one must start researching the peer-reviewed journals on the topic of interest within the discipline that one intends to investigate. The peer-reviewed literature search serves to establish what we already know, how the conclusions were arrived at, and their directions while identifying areas that require additional empirical research (Creswell, 2014). A gap in the literature may take several forms. Let us examine several types and provide examples of writing each gap. For example,

1. The gap in the literature is that although the literature has conceptually established that........(name, year; name, year; name, year), there has been no empirical study confirming this idea. [This case shows that there is consensus in the literature, but no empirical investigation has been conducted to verify the logic of the argument supported with field research].
2. The gap in the literature is that there are two sets of competing views in the literature, with one believing that......(name, year; name, year; name, year) while the

others believe that……..(name, year; name, year; name, year). [This gap helps establish which belief is correct by conducting empirical research].

3. The gap in the literature is that although various studies have investigated ……. qualitatively/quantitatively (name, year; name, year; name, year), they have not examined the issue quantitively/qualitatively. [This provides an opportunity to explore a gap with a different research design. Using a qualitative research design can supplement our knowledge of the same issue if a quantitative study has already been done and vice-versa].

The question which many ask is: how and where does one find a literature gap? The answer lies in a systematic review of the literature on peer-reviewed databases because a dissertation requiring empirical research should offer other investigators the opportunity to replicate it and confirm or reject the study. Therefore, as the first step, one must determine the relevant keywords. Second, based on the keywords and topic, one should identify the databases such as EBSCO or ProQuest that could yield a sufficient number of peer-reviewed journals to examine the breadth and depth of the phenomenon of interest.

There are two basic ways to search the literature: finding articles strictly by keywords or using the keywords and then applying a cascading process. In the first instance, one sees all the relevant articles based on the keywords to establish which gaps exist as we already described. When using the combination of keywords and cascading, after finding the articles based on the selected words, one uses the references from those articles to expand the search to grasp better the depth and breadth of the gaps, or other possible gaps that could not be discerned by just reviewing the keywords.

The identified gap must be compelling, engaging, expand academic knowledge, and have practical significance (Huff, 2009). Therefore, as discussed thus far, a gap in a Ph.D. dissertation should be rooted in the current literature, not a work problem. Furthermore, it would not be compelling if the gap simply intends to increase our understanding. The researchers should be aware that increasing one's understanding does not necessarily add to the current knowledge. After identifying the gap, the researcher will formulate a concise problem statement.

Strategy 2: Formulating Problem Statement

A problem statement should be concise, rooted in a literature gap, be researchable, positioned within a discipline and the domain of inquiry, and be socially relevant. The problem statement, when written concisely, should be two paragraphs. The first paragraph should explain the practical or social issues which are the symptoms of the problem. This paragraph should be three to four sentences, encapsulating the dissertation introduction and background. The second paragraph should include the general (the broader problem) and the specific problem based on the identified gap in the literature. Before one begins writing a problem statement, one should be mindful of the issues discovered when exploring the gap in the literature.

When writing a problem statement, the wording we use changes how one writes the purpose statement selecting a research design, impacting the feasibility and ethical issues that would be a concern for an ethical review board before we can proceed to collect data. We will expand on the wording in the problem statement later when we discuss alignment. Let us review some examples here while offering how to construct a problem statement.

Example 1:

Paragraph 1--Social/Practical issue:

Doctors have discovered that people with insomnia also suffer from……(Citations from professional magazines, newspapers). The doctors' observation has been corroborated by clinicians in several countries (citations from professional magazines, newspapers). Also, dentists have noticed that people with insomnia have a higher rate of bleeding when doing dental surgery (citation from professional magazines, newspapers).

Paragraph 2--General & specific problem paragraph

The general problem is that although the literature has addressed insomnia symptoms, its cause and effects have not been widely addressed (several citations from peer-reviewed journals to indicate a consensus about the issue). The specific problem is that the literature has not established a clear relationship between insomnia and blood pressure or bleeding (several citations from peer-reviewed journals to indicate a consensus about the issue).

Example 2:

Paragraph 1--Social/Practical issue:

Recidivism poses an unnecessary financial burden on society for the cost of repeated incarceration......(Citations from professional magazines, newspapers). Despite various attempts to reduce recidivism, the percentage of individuals facing repeated incarceration remains high (citations from professional magazines, newspapers). While some have blamed the officials, others remain convinced that there are no processes to reduce recidivism once they leave their incarceration (citation from professional magazines, newspapers).

Paragraph 2--General & specific problem paragraph

The general problem is that although the literature has addressed recidivism, it has not determined how processes may reduce it either inside the prison or once the offenders have completed their sentence (several citations from peer-reviewed journals to indicate a consensus about the issue). The specific problem is that the literature has not established how social processes could be improved after completing one's sentence to reduce recidivism (several citations from peer-reviewed journals to indicate a consensus about the issue).

As the two problem statements showed, we moved from the social or practice-based issue to the literature gap in both examples. Using the citation, we identified the specific problem based on a literature gap and ensured we had a consensus about the gap. The specific problem also offered us another clue—the research design.

When reviewing the specific problem in example 1, the relation between insomnia, blood pressure, and bleeding are present. The word *relation* would determine the type of research design, which would be quantitative. The specific problem presents an issue that requires investigating the relationship or some types of correlations. The word *relation* directs us to select particular research designs to investigate the issue. In the second example, the word *process* requires us to use a specific research design to explore the issue. We will address both instances more in depth when addressing the purpose statement. Before moving on, let us review whether these two examples are researchable, positioned within a discipline and the domain of inquiry, and be socially relevant.

Reviewing example one, one could gather sufficient material in the introduction and background of the study to articulate that insomnia is a social problem because it could impact productivity, individuals' health, etc. The line of argument establishes an adequate ground to justify its significance and the need for the study. Second, if the authors obtain their Ph.D. degrees in epidemiology, the topic falls within the discipline and the domain of inquiry. Finally, the problem is researchable, lending itself to empirical studies determining a relationship or lack of it between variables.

Reviewing the second example, one could gather sufficient material in the introduction and background of the study to articulate that recidivism is a social problem because it could impact productivity, individuals' social wellbeing, etc. The line of argument establishes an adequate ground to justify its significance and the need for the study. Second, if the authors obtain their Ph.D. degrees in sociology, management, anthropology, or other disciplines may use the topic depending on how they state the problem and relate it to their respective field. Finally, the problem is researchable, lending itself to empirical studies determining how to improve the processes or what dynamics might impact it.

Strategy 3: Writing the purpose statement

The purpose statement offers a concise, half-page length that connects the specific problem to the required research design to investigate it. The purpose statement should include: (a) the specific type of research design within a qualitative or quantitative scheme, (b) the study's intent by using terms such as describe, compare, correlate, explore, expound, and develop, and (c) the details of the research design, in brief, explaining the type of research design appropriate for data collection and analysis and, if quantitative, outlining the independent, dependent, and covariate variables. The purpose statement typically starts with a concise declaration about the type of research design. For instance, using the specific problem example from insomnia, we can state the purpose as follow:

> **Example 1:** The purpose of this quantitative study is to examine the relationship between insomnia as an independent variable and blood pressure and bleeding and explore any intervening or mediating factors. [Here, the researcher must add: (a) concisely the study variables, explain which is an independent, dependent, covariate, mediating, etc., as appropriate, (b) identify the research design and its connection to the research questions, (c) explain any types of constraints such as resource or time, and (d) describe how the research design selection is consistent with advancing knowledge in the discipline based on the specific problem. If conducting an intervention study, defend the choice of intervention.]

As a starting point for determining the range of available quantitative research designs, the readers are encouraged to review Martin and Bridgmon (2012) or similar research method textbooks and then, using its references, explore the in-depth opportunities each research design offers. The researchers should be mindful that the research design in a quantitative purpose statement must align with the wording in the problem statement. At the same time, consider the ethical implications for data collection in the specific problem. First, the purpose statement is always driven by the terms used in the specific research problem. Second, suppose the quantitative purpose statement indicated something about intervention in an experimental or quasi-experimental design. In that case, the researcher must consider the ethics review board clearance and the feasibility of data collection. Anticipating the obstacles before one face them is imperative to remain on schedule for completing a dissertation.

Turning our attention to a qualitative purpose statement, the wording used in the research problem dictates the specific types of qualitative research design. One must be mindful that each term in the problem statement leads to a particular type of research design, e.g., descriptive phenomenology, multiple case study, etc. There is always more than one type of research design that one may pursue. Before formulating the purpose statement, the researcher must pay close attention to the terms used in the problem statement and scan the range of possible research design options. In our recidivism example, the term *process* was used. When reviewing the possible research designs, the researcher should pay attention to the core of the problem, which is the *process*. Let us assume that the researcher intends to use one type of phenomenology, which is only applicable if we want to understand experiences, unfold meaning, or describe what has taken place. However, the word *process* requires understanding a system with its parts. In this scenario, a researcher may select either one type of case (see Yin, 2018 for a full explanation of case study design) or Delphi design (see Dalkey & Helmer-Hirschberg, 1962 for details). In our example, we must research a set of contemporary social phenomena, composing and creating the process, based on what the individuals involved know and how the internal and external organizational artifacts can corroborate (Yin, 2018). Therefore, one type of case study may be a feasible design to help us investigate the issue. If we decide to use a case study, then the example of our purpose statement would be as follow:

> **Example 2:** The purpose of this qualitative multiple case study is to explore social processes to help individuals after serving their sentences to reduce recidivism. [Here, the researcher must state: (a) concisely the phenomenon under investigation, (b) identify the research design and its connection to the specific research problem, (c) explain any types of constraints such as resource or time, and (d) describe how the research design selection is consistent with advancing knowledge in the discipline based on the specific problem. If observation of the sample population or vulnerable population sampling is required, they should be stated.]

As a starting point for determining the range of available qualitative research designs, the readers are encouraged to review Patton (2014) and then, using its references explore the in-depth opportunities each research design offers. The researchers must be mindful of possible options and associated work requiring time and resources. For example, it is possible to use Grounded Theory (see Corbin & Straussm, 2015) to investigate processes to reduce recidivism. However, the time and effort to complete the task, moving systematically between interpreting the data and referring to the literature in creating a new theory. This process requires (a) extensive literature review to ensure all dimensions of the issue are covered at each step and (b) a plausible valid theory is created. Because a Ph.D. candidate is a novice researcher and has limited time to complete the dissertation as the first scientific investigation, the more complicated research design should be delayed until after earning one's doctorate with less time pressure.

Each method serves a different purpose in a different context, some stretching the boundaries of qualitative methodology far beyond abductive reasoning. For example, Elliott and Timulak (2021), rooting their argument for research in psychotherapy, have argued that all qualitative research methods have some data collection and analysis instruments in common. Therefore, as Elliott and Timulak (2021) assessed the qualitative method, they concluded that one could use a generic qualitative method without explaining the contextual issues. Elliott and Timulak argued that "applying the same brand-name methodological approach to two studies by no means guarantees similarity of strategies and procedures" (p.9). The challenge is that when one applies a method, it is accompanied by a context, allowing for a particular viewpoint for data collection and analysis, bringing us to our next point—the differences in the contexts.

Phenomena are different. Some phenomena may deal with perception, some living experience, others with lived experiences, yet others may address dynamics, processes, or some of their parts. Therefore, each phenomenon requires a different method for its examination, and although they may have some common tools for data collection, they also possess others that are not common. Essentially, each research is nonlinear storytelling, bounded by the discipline, coherently argued by detailed data and its analysis (Golden-Biddle & Locke, 2007). Therefore, attention to the specific research problem wording is imperative in knowing how to use an appropriate method to study it. For example, understanding a process or dynamics in an organization may lend itself to a case or Delphi study. Each method requires different data collection instruments and analysis based on the research problem and the question is asking.

Strategy 4: Asking an Effective Research Question

The research question (RQ) in a dissertation should enable the researcher to investigate the specific research problem empirically and meaningfully. However, stating RQ is not straightforward and contains many parts (Maxwell, 1996). Research question requires (a) formulation to align with the theoretical or conceptual framework, based on the research method design, (b) validity through triangulation of its sources, theories in answering the question, and the literature within the same discipline, and (c) establish a relationship with the literature examined, and consideration for the time and resources for data collection and analysis (Maxwell, 1996).

Considering the requirements outlined for drafting an RQ, it should restate the specific research problem in the form of a question with particular attention to the overall research method—quantitative or qualitative. First, we will examine the quantitative RQ. In quantitative research design, the RQ must align with the specific research problem and the theoretical framework, allowing for a clear pathway for formulating the hypotheses and collecting and analyzing the data (Martin & Bridgmon, 2012). To develop hypotheses to answer the RQ correctly, we must identify the independent, dependent variables and their types. Here, the researcher must clearly state whether the independent variable is *active*/subject to manipulation or *attribute*/categorial and define the *extraneous* and *criterion* dependent variables (Martin & Bridgmon, 2012, pp.30-31). The clarification allows us to collect data based on pre-defined ideas, allowing accurate interpretation. We will provide the following example for formulating a quantitative research question regarding the insomnia problem.

Example 1:

The specific problem is that the literature has not established a clear relationship between insomnia and blood pressure or bleeding (several citations from peer-reviewed journals indicate a consensus about the issue).

RQ: (based on examining the relationship, as stated in the purpose), we could construct the RQ as follow: What is the relationship between insomnia as an independent variable and blood pressure and bleeding as dependent variables?

Note: one should remember that a theoretical frame is required in investigating the issue, and one may change the RQ based on the theoretical frame adopted for exploring the relationship. E.g., How does theory---- explain the relationship between insomnia as an independent variable and blood pressure and bleeding as dependent variables. The theoretical framework is required to provide a clear roadmap for data collection and analysis.

In Example 1, the wording and terms used in the research problem, the purpose, and RQ align, ensuring our investigation moves in the same direction. For instance, if the research problem were stating something about an experiment, we would have to change the wording in the RQ to ask a question consistent with the problem—aligned (Creswell, 2014, pp.142-3). In quantitative studies, once the RQ is developed, we should state the hypotheses to test possible outcomes—predictors. Therefore, for example 1, we must have a minimum of three hypotheses, of which one would be a null hypothesis.

Example 1

RQ: What is the relationship between insomnia as an independent variable and blood pressure and bleeding as a dependent variable?

Null Hypothesis: There is no significant relationship between insomnia, blood pressure, and bleeding.

Hypothesis 1: Insomnia increases as blood pressure and bleeding increase.

Hypothesis 2: Insomnia decreases as blood pressure and bleeding increase.

Given the limited financial and time constraints that individual doctoral research has, one should attempt to minimize the objectives of the research, its purpose, and what the RQ intends to find. In quantitative research, each question has a set of hypotheses requiring data collection and analysis of each set. Therefore, if there is more than one RQ, the researcher must (a) ensure each RQ aligns with the research problem and the purpose, and (b) each requires a set of hypotheses needing data collection and analysis. Therefore, more questions would lead to more complications while increasing the pressure on the researcher to deal with time and financial constraints to complete the project.

When posing qualitative RQs, close attention is required to its purpose about what specific *thing* we want to understand, what is the *significance* of knowing that, why is it *important to know* the answer, how will *go about learning* it, and *how feasible* would it be to investigate it (Maxwell, 2013). The wording in qualitative RQ can change the theoretical focus and its relationship to the conceptual framework (Maxwell, 2013).

Example 2:

The specific problem is that the literature has not explored social processes to help individuals after serving their sentences to reduce recidivism (several citations from peer-reviewed journals indicate a consensus about the issue).

RQ: (based on examining the relationship, as stated in the purpose), we could construct the RQ as follow: how social processes could be improved to reduce recidivism to help individuals after serving their sentences?

Note: one should remember that a conceptual frame is required in investigating the issue, and one may change the RQ based on the conceptual frame adopted for exploring the process. E.g., How does theory---- explain the social process improvement in recidivism reduction. The conceptual framework is required to provide a clear roadmap for data collection and analysis.

As noted, several points require attention as one states the RQ. First, the RQ wording must reflect what the investigation attempted, as previously stated in the problem and the purpose. Second, using synonyms for terms used in the problem and purpose might create an obstacle by suggesting a different meaning, leading one in another direction; hence, one should avoid it. Third, the researcher should avoid multiple RQs to avoid alignment problems and limit the time and resources required to collect, analyze, and publish the work. Fourth, if a researcher has more than one RQ, then more than one interview question set, or survey question set may be required to gather the necessary data. Therefore, the less RQ, the less work, and the dissertation project can move forward more expeditiously.

Strategy 5: Aligning Parts

The logic of any argument rests on the alignment of the parts in a dissertation. Usually, terms used in various parts provide signposts indicating the direction of the discussion (Creswell, 1994). More importantly, alignment should offer the reader a logical and cohesive argument unequivocally connecting the parts. As illustrated in Figure 1., elements from chapter 1 to the final chapter of a dissertation must align. The alignment requires focused attention to laying the groundwork in the introduction about the topic at hand, offering substantive background

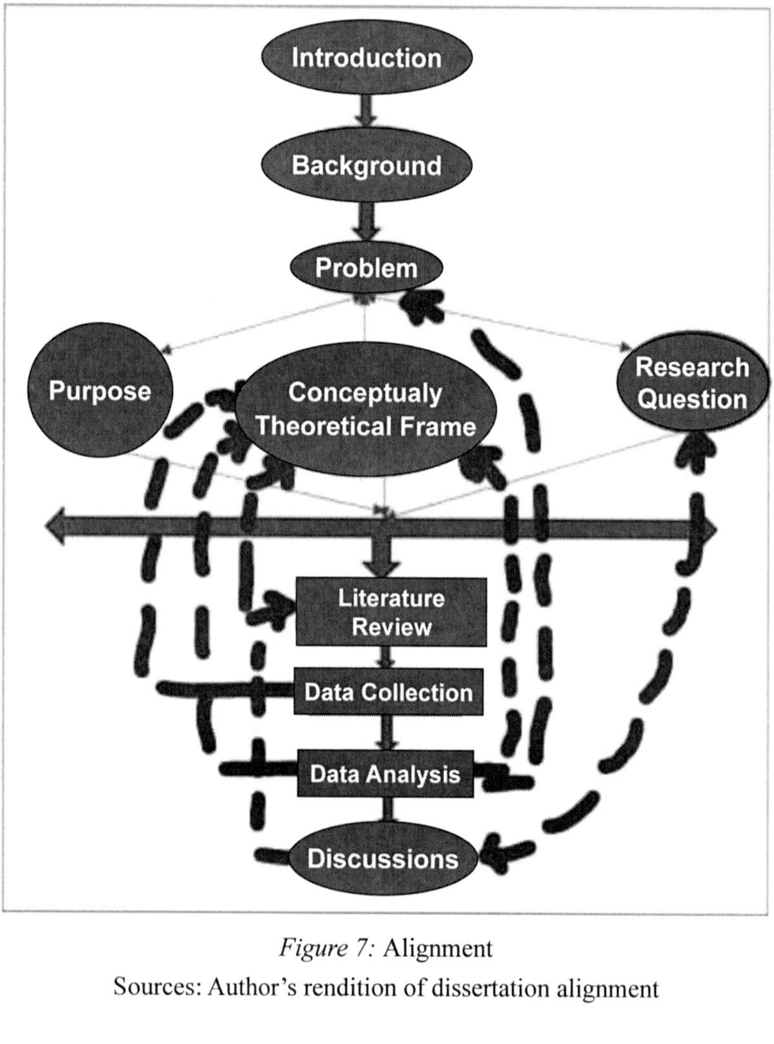

Figure 7: Alignment

Sources: Author's rendition of dissertation alignment

connecting the significance of the study based on the gap in the current peer-reviewed literature and practice, leading to the articulation of the specific research problem.

The research problem should align with (a) the purpose, addressing the research method design, (b) conceptual/theoretical framework, offering the data collection and analysis roadmap (the conceptual/theoretical framework should be consistent with the existing literature), and (c) research question guiding the researcher to find the answer to the specific research problem. While the RQ offers a clear understating of what the research is attempting to know, the purpose indicates how one would investigate the research problem. The conceptual/theoretical framework would let the reader understand the data collection and analysis roadmap. As the researcher arrives at the discussion stage to tie all work together, the section should refer back to the literature review for compare and contrasting findings to confirm or invalidate the current literature conclusions based on the conceptual/theoretical framework. If any of the steps described here are missed, the research would not be aligned, and its findings could be challenged for validity and reliability.

Strategy 6: Addressing the population

Dissertation research focuses incrementally on expanding the existing knowledge rooted in a current literature gap. Therefore, the research problem, purpose, and RQ should align and focus on the doctoral researcher's gap. The sample population that a dissertation selects to collect the data is not a part of the problem, purpose, or RQ; it is about which population provides the data. Therefore, the sample population is usually stated in the nature of the study in the first chapter.

In the nature of the study, the researcher should briefly (a) provide a concise rationale for selecting the design and tradition,

(b) describe the key study variables or the issue investigated, (c) summarize from whom and how data are collected and how the data will be analyzed. The nature of the study should clearly (a) define the target population, (b) the target population size or approximate (e.g., until saturation is reached in qualitative studies), (c) identify and justify the type of sampling strategy, (d) state procedures for how the sample will be drawn, (e) the inclusion and exclusion criteria, (f) any other required justification.

The doctoral researcher, in the nature of the study section, must also explicitly describe (a) the recruiting procedures and certain demographic information, (b) how informed consent will be provided to the participants, (c) how data will be collected, what the procedure would be for debriefing the participants, and (d) any follow-up procedures. Any pertinent information such as intervention should be stated in this section to afford the institution's Ethical Review Board to determine if the process meets all the ethical requirements. The details of the entire process, from contacting the participants, selection process, data collection, and any procedure in between, must be fully disclosed to maintain transparency for ethical issues that might require further review.

Strategy 7: Assumptions, limitations, and delimitations

Assumptions are aspects of the study that might be true but could not be demonstrated to be true. All assumptions require clarification and explanation. Aspects that are not pertinent or critical should be avoided. Only assumptions that are critical to the study meaningfulness should be included. The researcher should expound on the rationale for stating the limitations necessary for the research context.

Limitations explain aspects of the research problem that the study would focus on, outlining the investigation's boundaries.

Delimitations clarify the boundaries of the research by specifying which populations would be included or excluded and which theoretical or conceptual frameworks would be used as a roadmap for data collection and analysis—addressing the issue of external validity. The limitation also addresses (a) generalizability, (b) issues related to limitations of internal and external validity, construct validity, and confounding variables based on the study design and method, and (c) biases or issues that could affect the outcome of the study.

Strategy 8: Discussion of Findings and Recommendations

Discussions and findings in the final chapter of the dissertation offer an opportunity to state how we expanded, deepened, or broadened the knowledge, why, significance, and practical implications. Essentially, discussions will (a) describe how findings confirm, disconfirm, or extend knowledge in the discipline by comparing them with what has been found based on the peer-reviewed literature that the researcher has conducted, (b) analyze and interpret the findings based on the conceptual/theoretical framework, (c) limit the interpretations to the acquired data and findings based on the assumptions, limitations, and delimitation, (d) explain the limitations to its generalizability validity, and reliability, as described (typically in chapter 1).

When discussing the findings, depending on the research approach (quantitative or qualitative), the researcher should clearly outline any mitigating circumstances that might have changed the results and the significance of those issues. For example, if the researcher selected to conduct quantitative quasi-experimental research, what were its effects on the findings, and how the results might have been different should a chosen experimental design randomize the subjects.

Alternatively, suppose a qualitative case study was selected to explore processes or dynamics. In that case, the researcher should explain how selecting a Delphi seeking expert views through various iterations might have resulted in different findings.

The discussion section of the dissertation is a unique inflection point—from what we have known to what we still must know. When stated concisely, the discussions, based on reviewing the relevant literature review, limitations, scope, delimitations, and research method, open a window into offering recommendations for future studies. Recommendations should show what type of future studies should be conducted to address the shortcomings of the stated research findings understand other aspects that were not studied in the research or could not have been explored. Finally, the recommendation should note the possible implications of the study.

Implications should describe how the findings impact (a) the domain of inquiry within the discipline and the paradigm within which the topic had already been addressed, (b) the practice, and (c) the society. The implications should tie the conversation to the significance of the study that a researcher offers from Chapter 1. The looping back to the significance confirms the importance of the study to the reader.

Strategy 9: Citation authenticity

Doctoral candidates are aware of plagiarism and the importance of correctly citing and quoting based on the citation format requirements by their institution. Our point here is not focused on plagiarism but rather on the authenticity of paraphrasing to ensure accuracy. A recent technical editing review of medical journals revealed that 41% of citations contained inaccuracies (Luo et al., 2013), leading to several issues.

Lack of accuracy of citing another work typically leads to loss of trust by the reader in what is presented, may result in invalidating the argument made by the researcher, and throws the entire study into doubt. As Aksnes et al. (2019) argued, citation accuracy gives the topic of inquiry plausibility and credibility to the work's origin under investigation. The accuracy of origin and plausibility points lead us to the next issue—the stated gap. If the researcher simply attempted to make the gap's existence real by distorting or inaccurately reflecting the original claim, everything else in the study would fall apart like a house of cards. It is incumbent upon the researcher to ensure the gap, which is the basis of the problem, leads to the research question, and the study is on solid ground. Therefore, authentically citing the work would lead to a solid foundation, the gap that drives the rest of a dissertation. However, the gap is only one part of the dissertation, and inaccurate, inauthentic citations could impact any part of the dissertation giving rise to other issues.

Each part of a dissertation builds on the work of others in expanding, broadening, or deepening knowledge. Therefore, in addition to the gap, the research problem statement, the purpose, the conceptual/theoretical framework, and the literature review build on what others have done and how authentic the work of others have been reflected to convey the correct meaning of others' work correctly. Therefore, it is essential that the researcher correctly cite others' work to ensure the study is built on a sound foundation. Its processes are validated. The findings are measured, compared, and contrasted against the literature accurately in arriving at its results. The following example illustrates the issue of inaccurate citation.

Collet (2019) used transcendental phenomenology to examine the experiences of general education teachers. She then cited Moustakas's (1994) transcendental model attempts to investigate the shared experiences of educators. In her effort, Collet (2019) presented two inauthentic citations. First transcendental phenomenology may explain faith-based issues or be an appropriate research design for examining texts such as Bible but would not be suitable for experiences. After all, transcendental phenomenology rests on the text and structure of the phenomenon, as Moustakas (1994) explained. Therefore, when the research design is incorrectly cited and applied, the dissertation's investigation is flawed, and the results are invalid.

Strategy 10: Positive Mindset

Unlike undergraduate or graduate courses where learning outcomes are identified proactively by the professor, and there are activities to achieve those learning activities with appropriate rubrics and guidance, dissertation objectives and what it would do entirely depends on the researcher. Therefore, the shift in the burden of preparing the guidelines, setting the parameters, identifying the expected outcomes could be an overwhelming endeavor. However, there are steps that any doctoral researcher could take to remain positive through the process to complete the work. Although there are no single ways to maintain a positive mindset for completing a dissertation, the ten steps identified below help you through the process.

Step 1: The researchers should remember that they initiated the study. Hence, it is their responsibility to give the work equal weight to anything else they are doing during that period in their lives. For example, if the researcher is a mid-level executive in an organization, that position is not the only priority; the dissertation has equal weight. The recognition would allow one to reorient oneself positively to ensure the dissertation project is a project that requires completing just anything else at one's work.

Step 2: Anticipate life obstacles such as weddings, death, accidents, sickness, etc., that may hinder the progress. The doctoral candidates should allow for unforeseen circumstances and, like a project manager, should allow for the lag in delivery of a section of the work somehow. The doctoral candidate should realistically evaluate the situation and think that one cannot control unforeseen events. Still, one could control the timeline for completing the dissertation. Therefore, one should remain on task to complete the dissertation rather than be paralyzed by events while recognizing them and facing them.

Step 3: Before starting the dissertation process, one should have a conversation with their immediate family and close friends, seek their support, explain their possible absence from many of the social events in the short term, and seek their support for the road ahead. Building support among family and friends brings in the immediate support circle who can provide a source of cheer as one completes various parts of the dissertation and minimizes distractions.

Step 4: Build an academic support network. Depending on your field, such as the Psychology Association, Academy of Management, etc., becoming a member of the academic circles would enable you to develop a support network. The academies typically have mentorship programs and offer doctoral colloquia, providing different ways to review and support your dissertation endeavors.

Step 5: Celebrate completing each part of the work completed. As a doctoral candidate, you are your cheerleader. Acknowledge and recognize completion of each element, such as Chapter 1, obtaining approval from your ethical review board, etc. The celebration allows you to see what you have accomplished and offers a milestone that has been conquered, helping you see the possibilities getting closer by completing each part.

Step 6: Remain in tune with your dissertation committee members. They want your success. Your dissertation committee offers you feedback to help you complete your dissertation. Therefore, work with them, understand what they are attempting to tell you, take advantage of their feedback to move forward.

Step 7: Develop healthy habits to minimize stress. Avoid activities and situations that cause you distress and create a negative mindset. A doctoral candidate should develop a positive attitude by remaining focused on the dissertation at hand and avoiding negative thoughts. One way to stay positive is to avoid stressing over things with no control. Instead, try to do something that you can control.

Step 8: Seek completion, not perfection. The dissertation is not one's lifelong project. A dissertation demonstrates that following scientific and objective principles, one could expand, broaden, or deepen the knowledge within a given paradigm. Therefore, from the beginning of the dissertation, narrowing the scope of your problem, and focusing on a tiny issue, help you complete the work faster with fewer resources in a shorter time.

Step 9: Envision the future with Ph.D. possibilities and focus on it. Reorienting one's thoughts about how the degree could help achieve the things one wants to accomplish is an integral part of the process. Therefore, focusing on the limitless possibilities by earning your doctoral degree could help you remain motivated to complete faster.

Step 10: Keep reaching for the sky while keeping your foot on the ground. While envisioning the big picture about what you can do with your Ph.D., remain focused on completing small tasks associated with your dissertation to lead you to the finishing line

Hamid H. Kazeroony is an Extraordinary Professor at North-West University, South Africa, has taught various international executive programs, and is currently a Senior Contributing faculty at Walden University Management Ph.D. program and Professor at Minnesota State. He has published widely on management education, research methods, ethics, gender, and diversity. He is a frequent presenter for doctoral seminars in Europe, Africa, and Asia. Hamid has served as AOM Membership Committee member 2012-2013 and Membership Committee chair 2015-2019. Hamid has served at the European Academy of Management as GRDO program chair and Strategic Interest Group chair 2015-2020, and at Africa Academy of Management as Professional Development Workshop track chair, 2014-2020. Hamid is currently serving as a European Academy of Management Board member.

References

- Aksnes, D. W., Langfeldt, L., & Wouters, P. (2019). Citations, Citation Indicators, and Research Quality: An Overview of Basic Concepts and Theories. *SAGE Open*. https://doi.org/10.1177/2158244019829575

- Collet, J. D. (2019). *A Transcendental Phenomenology of General Education Teachers' Experiences Instructing Twice-exceptional High School Students* (Order No. 27544986). Available from ProQuest Dissertations & Theses Global. (2321833466). https://www.proquest.com/dissertations-theses/transcendental-phenomenology-general-education/docview/2321833466/se-2?accountid=14872

- Corbin, J., & Straussm A. (2015). Basics of Qualitative Research: Techniques and Procedures for Developing Grounded Theory (4th ed.). Sage.

- Creswell, J. W. (1994). *Research design: Qualitative and quantitative approaches.* SAGE.

- Creswell, J. W. (2014). *Research design: Qualitative, quantitative, and mixed methods approach* (4th ed.). SAGE.

- Dalkey, N.C. & Helmer-Hirschberg, O. (1962). An Experimental Application of the Delphi Method to the Use of Experts, Rand Corporation, Santa Monica, CA.

- Elliott, R., & Timulak, L. (2021). *Essentials of descriptive-interpretive qualitative research: A generic approach.* American Psychological Association.

- Golden-Biddle, K., & Locke, K. (2007). *Composing qualitative research.* Sage Publications.
- Huff, A.S. (2009). *Designing Research for Publication.* Sage.
- Kazeroony, H. & Du Plessis, Y. (2021). *The Ph.D. Mindset.* Information Age Publishing, Charlotte, NC. USA.
- Luo, M., Li., C.C., Molina, D., Andersen, C.R., & Panchbhavi, V.K. (2013). Accuracy of citation and quotation in foot and ankle surgery journals. *Foot Ankle Int. 34*(7), 949-55. doi: 10.1177/1071100713475354
- Martin, W.E. & Bridgmon, K. D. (2012) Quantitative and Statistical Research Methods: Research Methods for the Social Sciences. Wiley. Kindle Edition.
- Maxwell, J.A. (1996). *Qualitative Research Design: An Interactive Approach.* Sage publications, Thousand Oaks, CA.
- Maxwell, J. A. (2013). Qualitative Research design: An Interactive Approach (3rd. Ed.). Sage publications, Thousand Oaks, CA.
- Moustakas, C. (1994). *Phenomenological research methods.* Thousand Oaks, CA: Sage
- Patton, M. Q. (2014). *Qualitative research & evaluation methods: Integrating theory and practice.* Sage publications, Thousand Oaks, CA.

❒

Dr. Raghu's Top 10

1. Anyone can do a Ph.D

PhD is intensive and uniquely challenging which requires at least three years of constant hard work, dedication, and patience. Having said that, PhD is also an extremely rewarding program as it allows you to make genuine contribution to the field's knowledge system and produce new base for the future researchers to build on. As the highest level of academic qualification, PhD is the gateway to a new world of information and scholarship. It will allow you to understand any problem in depth and offer alternate explanations.

For many, PhD has had somewhat of a mystical status. It is often associated with geniuses and believed to have been only accomplished by a certain class of intellectually superior people. However, this cannot be far from the truth. In order to do PhD, one simply needs to be dedicated enough in their field of study and resilient enough to endure the rigorous process. Any who demonstrate qualities like intellectual curiosity, patience, resilience, and ability to solve problems, discipline and many more.

If your mind is resolved to do a PhD then accomplishing it can be quite easy. However, one must develop and hone certain qualities that will allow it be an easy and effortless process. The chances of you accomplishing a PhD are mostly dependent on your perseverance, hard work, and tenacity than on actual course work! So don't fret, you can and will do a PhD!

2. Dissertation is about Read & Write Exercise

Most doctoral students are extremely talented and excited about pursuing a research degree. They show tremendous potential and willingness to improve and hone their research skills. Once the initial excitement for the research subsides, the fear of the final dissertation creeps in. They are like the two sides of a coin and can't be separated. It is what makes it such a unique experience. In all these years, my advice to the students has stayed the same. Don't worry about getting it right, get it written!

Dissertation is a reading and writing exercise. Reading expands your knowledge base and writing helps you put your thoughts constructively. Both of which are an extremely integral part of dissertation. The more you read, the more you should write. This reading and writing gives you time to think and gather your thoughts to formulate into an idea. I strongly believe that writing crystallizes your thoughts. It gives clarity and lucidity to your ideas. As a researcher, you have a wide range of ideas but they never appear to be good enough. They appear unclear because you haven't written them into existence. Once you write them down, you give them a new dimension where there is scope for further exploration.

You must not worry about drafting a perfect piece of scholarly article at the first go. Start by outlining your main ideas and elucidating with examples or explanations. As you write, there will be free flow of ideas and you will be a step closer to writing an insightful scholarly paper yourself. It is important that you don't wait for the perfect paper to be written but write it instead!

As a graduate student, the biggest challenge is writing your dissertation. To write a good dissertation, one must research, read and write. When students approach me with their research idea, I always ask them to write about it. Writing about the topic makes them think of it in a different light, which wouldn't have been possible just talking about it. Once they have made their mind about a topic, I advise my students to get into the habit of writing every day. It will enable you to become a prolific writer with well-organized and constructive ideas. It will simplify the dissertation writing process into a less stressful and rather enjoyable one.

It is imperative for any graduate researcher to write every day because writing is thinking. Quite often, graduate students procrastinate and wait for their 'Eureka' moment when ideas would flow into paper. But, that's never the case. Any good piece of writing is a product of several drafts. It is absolutely crucial to keep a written record of your ideas and thoughts because anything that is written can be improved and developed. If you follow a writing routine, you will have the opportunity to enhance it and make it better. So instead of simply thinking about it or discussing with your fellow researchers, get in the habit of writing. You will be surprised to see how this habit will help you in writing your final dissertation or any scholarly article.

Due to the tedious nature of research work, you will often find yourself frustrated and worried. Writing helps overcome these emotions and makes you feel confident about your ideas and observations. Writing gives you a chance to express your thoughts in an organized and constructive manner. The more you write the better it gets. With practice and patience, you'll find yourself writing an intelligent and coherent dissertation. PhD can be easy. All you need to do is, read and write!

3. Dissertation should be about 200+ Pages

Every doctoral student at some point of his or her PhD is faced with the question of, "How long should a dissertation be?" The answer is: as many as it takes, but within the university regulations or departmental limits. There is no right or wrong answer to this question. I believe it depends on various little details and the answer is quite subjective. There is no ideal number of pages in a dissertation.

Today, students have Internet to access a wide range of information, knowledge, and opinions that are relevant to the topic. This helps students enhance their study by making reference to others' works instead of a tightly argued and presented summary of their own ideas and achievements. These references are a must and take up a lot pages in the dissertation. However, many seem to think that quantity is the main determinant of grades. Thus, certain academics centres have had to impose word or page limits. In my over two decades of experience, I have supervised over 1000 dissertations. In order to gain an overall idea, I suggest students to look at different dissertations available in their area of study – at least ten of them. After closely working with students, I have come to a conclusion that the doctoral degree must be 200 pages or more.

Now that we have a general idea about the number of pages in dissertation, I want to clarify it further. Let me provide you an approximate number of pages that should be dedicated to each chapter:

- Chapter 1: 25+ pages
- Chapter 2: 50+ pages
- Chapter 3: 40+ pages
- Chapter 4: 40+ pages
- Chapter 5: 25+ pages

A dissertation does not have a definitive word limit. Different universities have different rules with regard to the length of a dissertation. However, the length depends on various factors like the number of pre-existing peer-reviewed research available in the topic. The length also differs based on your subject or topic. Keeping all this in mind, the doctoral dissertation is in all likelihood will be over 200 pages. While writing a dissertation, the focus should be on creating a comprehensive and quality research study instead of worrying about the length of this document.

4. Remember about 5 Chapter Model

Research must be methodological and written in such a way that it is easy for the reader to understand. Structure your work and findings in a logical order. In order to do so, you must avoid writing in a continuous prose form. Instead, divide your work into chapters and sections. When you are writing your thesis, split the work into 5 chapters and when you are writing a paper for publication there should be 5 sections.

What are these 5-Chapters?

1. **Introduction:** An introduction should state the topic; provide a context and rationale behind your choice. You introduce your reader to this area of study and explain, giving reasons as to why this study is important. You also write the problem statement and the goal of your study. This section is extremely important as it sets the tone of your work and hence it often takes longer to write. You should not rush into it. Make sure that the problem statement provides evidence that the problem is current and relevant to the discipline. You should clearly state the problem that the study is going to investigate. State your research questions or hypotheses. The goal statement should answer the question— what are you going to do

about the problem? End this section by outlining the major sections/chapters of the paper.

2. **Literature review:** The second chapter requires you to present a review of scholarly literature related to your study. It is important to situate your research in the larger framework of available literature. The main idea is to present, summarize, compare and contrast research relevant to your study. The literature that you address should be current and support your problem and goal statement in some way. One of the common misconceptions among students is that literature review is about simply summarizing books and articles. This is not true. You must be able to write a focused review and explain how it is related to your area of research. A good literature review will convince the reader that the study addresses some important questions and adds to the understanding of the topic by offering a new perspective.

3. **Methodology:** This section deals with the method or technique you use to identify and analyze information applied to understand the research problem. There are two major questions that this section needs to answer.

    1. How the data was collected?
    2. How was it analyzed?

    Methodology is an important section because an unreliable method produces incorrect and unreliable results. There are many different methods for investigation of a research problem and you should explain the reasons for choosing a particular procedure or technique. When you choose the method, it should be able to fulfill the aim of the study.

4. **Results:** This section deals with reporting the findings of your study. Based on your research, you confirm or reject

the hypothesis and/or answer your research questions. It is important that you provide data and the analysis related to your study. Avoid including unnecessary data that are not critical to answering your research question. This section is basically about narrating your findings without trying to evaluate or interpret them.

5. **Summary, conclusion, and further research:** This section is extremely important as it shows how well you have developed your argument or answered the questions. Here, you will start by summarizing the key finding of your study. Additionally, you will analyze and interpret the finding in the theoretical and conceptual framework. You will also suggest the implication of your finding. Every research paper should open avenues for further study. A good research paper leaves behind a few ideas for other researchers to work on. Finally, you should write a well-crafted conclusion—the final word on your research. It should be a strong message that reflects on the essence of the study.

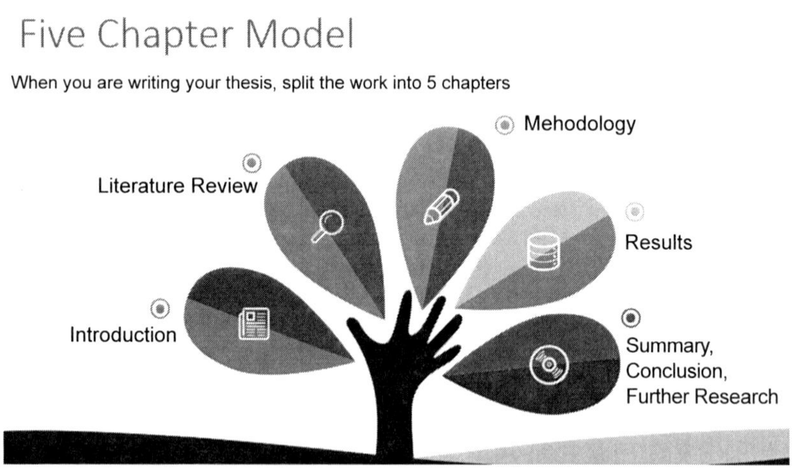

Figure 8: Five Chapter Model

These were the five major parts of any kind of academic writing, especially doctoral dissertation. In addition to these key chapters, there are two other sections-- titled 'Abstract' before the first chapter and 'References' at the end, after chapter 5. As novice researchers, you will have to be mindful of these aspects of research writing. Following this format will enable you to write papers with more clarity and fluency. Follow the 5-chapter model for a 5-star research paper!

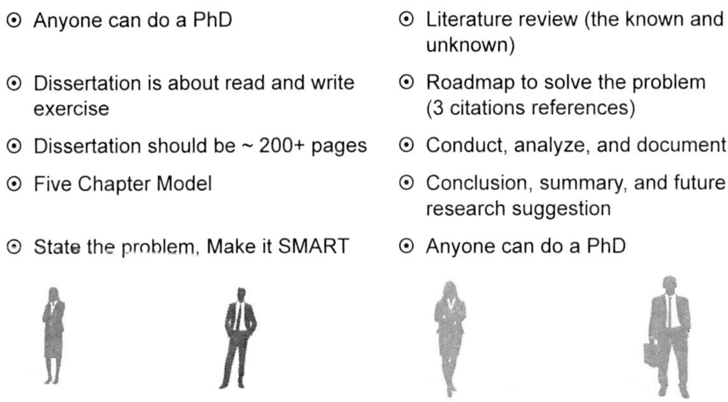

Figure 9: Top 10 Considerations While Pursuing a PhD

5. State the Problem: Make it SMART (25+ Pages)

Like any written document, start your academic research paper with an Introduction. It is generally the first paragraph but in case of research writing, it must be longer and have various subsections. Ideally in a doctoral thesis, it should be 25 pages or more. It should give a background, state your problem statement, give an overview of the nature, significance and purpose of the study etc.

You start your introduction by providing general idea of the topic in question and then give your thesis statement that is central to your study. An Introduction is singled handedly the most important part of your thesis or research paper as it familiarizes the reader with the core ideas of your study. Writing an introduction is often considered the most challenging part of writing a paper. Therefore, I always advise my students to write the introduction in the end as it gives you time to organize your thoughts. Additionally, if there are changes during your research, you don't have to keep going back to your introduction and modify it.

Start your introduction by declaring the problem statement. The problem statement is the heart of any research paper. It is a short, usually a paragraph long section detailing the key problem that is worthy of study. It is an extremely important part of the study; if the problem statement is week then the whole study will be compromised. There are two stages to the process of writing a problem statement: Arriving to a problem statement and writing a problem statement.

How to get to a problem statement?

In order to narrow down your study from a vague topic or a question to a specific research problem, you need to do a thorough review of the literature. This activity will enable you to find out the gaps, which needs to be filled. It will reveal what you don't know and needs to be found. Researchers believe that you cannot answer a question that only intrigues you. It must be a problem whose solution will be crucial to your research community.

How to write a problem statement?

Discuss with your committee chair (Guide), they will guide you through your problem statement. There is no template for writing a problem statement. It is usually a paragraph or two long and not more than that. You can start with a simple and direct sentence talking about what problem the study addresses. You should include answers to the following "W's":

- What is the problem?
- Who does the problem affects?
- What method will be used to solve the problem?
- Why is it important to fix the problem?
- What are the possible outcomes, if the problem was not solved?

If these questions are answered in a logical and sequential manner, then you'll have a comprehensive problem statement.

A problem statement should be SMART. It is an acronym for specific, measurable, achievable, realistic, and tangible. A good problem statement should be all of these things.

1. **Specific:** Avoid generic problem statements. It must provide a well-defined and precise problem. It must not be unnecessarily too elaborate.
2. **Measurable:** It must measure the progress towards the goal of fixing the problem.
3. **Achievable:** The problem statement must show that the solution to the problem is attainable.
4. **Realistic:** Make sure your problem statement is grounded in reality and is accurate. It should showcase that you have the sensible idea of what can be achieved. The dissertation or thesis is usually done within 18 months
5. **Tangible:** The problem statement should be something that touches your heart.

A problem statement is stepping stone in your research writing. It should be designed in such a way that every aspect of the problem is addressed. But, it shouldn't be too long with too many details and descriptions. It must be **SMART**, short, and concise. A problem statement helps you stay focused on your research and to create more organized project. Remember your W's and you'll have a problem statement ready in no time!

A good way to start your problem statement is to study "Further Research opportunities" on your area of interest.

One of those further research opportunities can be your problem statement.

6. Literature review: the known & unknown (50+ Pages)

Literature review is the most misperceived chapter in research. It is considered to be the chapter about citations and quotations from different sources but it is not the case. Literature review is much more than just making random references and citations, Literature review is an amalgamation of what is known and what is unknown. It is a story that a researcher narrates and it is a roadmap to his study. It is one of the longest chapters in your thesis. It must be more than 50 pages of insightful and well-researched description of relevant literature.

Every research study is a body of knowledge system, which is a composition of known and unknown facts and items. A researcher has a set of facts and assumptions on which he bases his study. And there are certain unknown facts and controversial aspects that the researcher finds during the process of background study. In a subsection titled 'Gap in Literature', before the 'Summary and Conclusions', the researcher logically synthesizes the known and the unknown items. A strong literature review will have an amalgamation of known and unknown items. The known items are aspects that you are aware of and your research is based on it. Unknown items are the gaps in the knowledge system that you would like to address in your study. This section should address the impact of the known and unknown items over the body of knowledge. In order words, you should explain how your study would influence the field. Will it add breadth to the scholarship and if so, how will it do so? It is important to write it in such a way that it expresses the need to research the unknown through the known items. Writing this section will help the readers understand the need for your study.

Writing a literature review is like mapping the terrain for your readers. It is a composition of ideas that are aligned to your problem and purpose statement. You provide a series of conceptual or theoretical framework that pertains to your study and provides a background to your research. In order to make a strong foundation to your study, you must cite from a few relevant sources. Ideally, a literature review should have the most recent and current reference. 80% of the citations should be from the last 5 years and the rest 20% can be older and seminal works. These references cannot be randomly included into the literature review.

There is a structure that must be followed and organized in a logical order. Your literature review must be divided into paragraphs and each paragraph must be organized in the following manner:

1. Identify the main topic of the paragraph and describe this main idea in some detail.
2. Once you have identified the main idea then provide relevant citation to support it. In research an idea cannot sustain alone, it must be reinforced with the help of suitable citation.

3. Next, analyze the topic discussed in this paragraph. With the help of the citation form a connection with the topic. Explain the topic in detail and how it is relevant to problem and purpose of your research.
4. Finally, give a transition statement to the next topic. Each paragraph should end with a sentence or two relating the ideas in one paragraph to the next.

These steps ensure that the literature review is written in a logical and organized manner and is not a random cluster of citations. Literature review is all about creating a background for your study. It helps the readers to understand the theoretical and conceptual origin of your research. While you write the review, you must be conscious of the fact that it cannot be a mere document of quotations or citations. It should be a comprehensive and insightful record that is well structured and organized. A literature review is weak if it doesn't address the impact of known and unknown aspects of research on the body of knowledge. Literature review is strong when it makes a connection between the known and lesser-known variables. It should address the gap in literature and how the study will contribute in existing body of knowledge in the area of study. Remember, a literature review must answer the questions: who said what and how is it related to the problem?

To help you start on Literature Review—better to start "Annotated Bibliography". To understand it better, here is an extract from one of my own works (Korrapati, 2016):

An annotated bibliography is a list of citations to books, articles, and documents. Each citation is followed by a brief (usually about 150-200 words) descriptive and evaluative paragraph - the annotation. The purpose of the annotation is to inform the reader of the relevance, accuracy, and quality of the sources cited.

Annotated Bibliography, like most written documents, has a structure. It is usually a page-long text consisting of a summary of the main ideas presented in a particular study. It does not have a title; instead, the APA citation of that particular article/research paper goes on the top of the page. The following subsections then follow it:

1. **The Problem:** Here, you must discuss the key problem addressed in the paper or study in question.
2. **Primary Source:** If the study is based on a particular idea or an existing work by some other scholar, then it is mentioned in this section. If not, then this section can be ignored.
3. **Methodology Used:** Describe the method adopted and implemented by the researcher.
4. **Results:** Briefly discuss the results and outcome of the study.
5. **Further Research Possibilities:** List out prospective research ideas and possibilities for further research.

7. Methodology: Roadmap to Solve the Problem: 3 Citations References (25+ Pages)

Research is an intense creative process, involving both analysis, in which you take things apart, and synthesis, in which you put things together. Your unique product will be the result of your individual thinking and incorporation of existing scholarly work in your topic. Building a research roadmap is a process where you trace the developments in your area of interest and how that led you to work on the topic. A research roadmap, also known as the body of knowledge, is a unique document that is designed to provide an overview of the developments in the research area. A research roadmap helps the researcher to comprehensively articulate different advances in field of interest as well as position his research within a larger framework. The process of developing a doctoral research requires you to revisit all the seminal research papers, books, journals etc. that you read related to your study. While rereading them pay close attention to major developments and Research requires an individual to have in-depth knowledge of the topic in question and a passion to pursue it for further exploration. Before the researcher is involved in performing the research, he/she should spend time understanding the topic and in choosing a research method. A research cannot stand independently; it must make allusions to other existing studies to validate it. It is important to justify your choice with at least three citations.

In a research study, you have a wide range of research approaches. There is no right or wrong in research and you have the liberty to choose a method that you think best suits your study. However, you must be able to provide valid justification for your choice. You must cite at least three references. You should make use of the references related to your study in order to strengthen your claim. An assertion without any valid support is usually considered weak and incomplete.

No matter what research study you decide to use—qualitative, quantitative or mixed method, it should be supported by 2-3 references. The references don't necessarily have to be from three different sources for citation; it can be from one particular source. While using these references for justifications, you should phrase it in such a way that it is not exactly like the original -- avoid plagiarism. A wholesome research is the one that not only has an appropriate research method but also is backed up by strong explanations and justification.

To help you understand it better, here is an extract from one of my own works (Korrapati & Rapaka, 2009):

A descriptive survey will be used to collect information on and document the data required for the study. A descriptive survey is most commonly used when the researcher wants to study a current day condition or phenomenon (Leedy & Ormrod, 2005). This is as opposed to a historical analysis that seeks to understand events or conditions of the past. A descriptive survey may be an option for this study because the researcher sought to understand the current perceptions about factors that contribute to software project success from project managers and project stakeholders. Looking at current feelings and perceptions was important to the study because one of its intents was to compare the information collected here to past results published by the Standish Group. Knowing how project managers and project stakeholders once felt about contributing factors to project success would be of no use in trying to determine if those perceptions have changed since the Standish Group report was published in 1994. Survey research can be conducted in a number of ways. One way is to interview participants directly. This can be done face-to-face or via telephone. Another way to conduct survey research is through a self-administered Questionnaire. This method involves sending a questionnaire to the survey participants, asking them to complete it, and return it to the researcher. Survey research has its strengths and weaknesses. One of its strengths is that survey research is easy to design (Leedy & Ormrod, 2005).

In a research study, you'll make assertions with regard to the choice of your research method. While you make these claims, you must provide suitable explanation by justifying those using relevant works by other researcher. Supporting your choice for the research model with citations makes it stronger and proves that it is current and relevant to the field. Always cite at least three references to support your choice of research method.

8. Results: Do it and Document: Conduct, Analyze & Document (50+ Pages)

Once you have established your problem statement and provided enough supporting matter to back up your thesis question, it is time to do what you set out to do— conduct, analyze and document your study. Define the broad philosophical underpinning to your chosen research methods. Describe the rationale for the application of specific procedures and technique used to identify, select and analyze information applied to understand the research problem. In the chapter on methodology, you give an insight into the process of conducting, analyzing, and documenting the whole research. Therefore this chapter is usually over 50 pages long. It is essential that no shortcuts are made in writing this chapter as the reader evaluates the validity of the data presented here.

There are broadly three key types of methodology used in research—qualitative, quantitative and mixed methods. Based on your approach, the chapter is structured. An effective written methodology section should:

1. Introduce the overall methodological approach to investigating your research problem. Inform your readers about the approach you are adopting—qualitative, quantitative or mixed method.
2. Indicate how the research approach fits the research design. The method that you adopt should have a clear connection with your research problem.
3. Provide a background and rationale for the methodology used. It is important to provide an explanation to help readers understand the logic behind your choice.
4. Provide an explanation and justification for sample selection. A description of how and why was the sample chosen needs to be specified.

5. Explain the specific method of data collection you will implement.
6. Explain the data analysis technique.
7. Describe potential limitations that can affect your data collection process. Also explain how you are going to address them.

In addition to the above mentioned elements, there are a few aspects that you must be conscious of while writing your methodology:

- Use descriptive writing approach.
- Do not include your questionnaires, interview transcripts etc. They must be included in the appendices.
- Be direct and precise, and use the past tense.
- Include enough information so that the reader can judge the validity of the study.

The way you conduct, analyse, and document your research is reflective of the quality of your research. This chapter is dedicated to explain the readers the approach adopted to find answers to the research questions. Divided into section, the chapter highlights the method implemented to collect data and conduct data analysis. A well laid out and logical methodology can act as a backbone for the entire research study and help you shape an extremely strong results section. Therefore, dedicate enough time in conducting as well as documenting the findings.

9. Conclusion, Summary & Future Research Suggestions (25+ Pages)

Conclusion, Summary and further research suggestions is said to be the easiest chapter. In the previous chapters or sections, researcher tends to refer back and forth to the information highlighted in the other chapters. But in this chapter, you don't need to refer to the previous parts of the research. This is a comprehensive and independent chapter. This is a standalone chapter because it is a combination of chapter one, two, three, and four. It is where the whole thesis comes together through a summary and concluding remarks. This provides final take away messages and is about 25 pages long.

It is extremely crucial as it provides the reader with the summary of the entire study. It can independently explain the entire study to its reader. It is a chapter that is comprehensive and reiterates the story from chapters one, two, three, and four. It has subsections within the chapter that covers important aspects of the study. It is the concluding section and enlightens the reader about the conclusion drawn from the study. This chapter creates the opportunity for further research.

Through the summary you provide an overview of the whole study. This is aligned with the problem statement, purpose of the study, and the research questions of the study.

Through a conclusion, you take your reader to a new level of understanding about the thesis. A simple summary of your analysis is not satisfactory. You must enlighten your readers about your deductions, which is aligned to the problem statement and answers your research questions. In your conclusion you must also justify your reasons for choosing a particular research method and how it helped you answer the research questions.

Recommendation for further study is a subsection where the researcher provides ideas to broaden the scope of research in a particular topic. Ideas are presented and discussed in this section to help the researchers in the field to enhance the understanding to the topic. As a researcher, you must follow a few key pointers in order to avoid irrelevant recommendations. Writing detailed recommendations are highly recommended!

10. Anyone can do a PhD

If the last nine points have highlighted anything, it is that, with a structured approach and hard work, anyone can complete a PhD degree. Once you put your mind to it, there is nothing that you cannot achieve! A doctoral degree is no different, you have to have the right motivation, commit to your research and eliminate all distractions.

When you have a clear understanding of your research topic and its objective, adopting a few strategies will further strengthen your resolve to complete the PhD degree:

- Work with patience, perseverance, and diligence
- Be independent in your thoughts/actions
- Practice discipline, self-control, and time management
- Work on your problem solving ability and creativity
- Hone your intellectual curiosity
- Write one page every day.
- Eliminate self-sabotaging behaviours
- Write as much as you read
- Don't give up
- Build your mind and body

Unlike popular belief, PhD is not a mythical or unachievable goal. It is a simple and can be easily done if you are prepared to invest a significant amount of time, energy and effort. Choose your topic of interest, commit to see it through, act on your commitment everyday and you will see that PhD is actually easily achievable!

❑❑❑

Final Thoughts

Having completed many PhD degrees myself and supervised as well as mentored over a 1000 students over the past 22 years, I have always encouraged anyone who aspires to pursue PhD. To many, PhD appears to be a distant dream and only reserved for a certain group of intellectuals. This is not true. It only appears unachievable if you approach it with a conflicted mind. Simply focus on your end goal in your mind and say it out loud—I want to do a PhD and so I will.

In order to succeed in anything, one must find the will within and prepare a roadmap to finish line. Similarly, when you choose to do PhD, figure out what is the driving factor and use that to your advantage. Use that to get in front of a computer to write one page a day. One page has four paragraphs and each paragraph has 4 to 5 sentences. Remember to write as much as you read. Doing this may not come easily. You may want to give up. But always remember what your end goal is— to walk out with a PhD degree!

Passion, inquisitiveness, inventiveness, discipline, persistence, patience, and meticulousness are the most critical prerequisites for pursuing a successful PhD program. Deep dive within yourself and find all the trials and tribulations you need to go through to achieve your goal. Commit to your dream and you will see those wonderful three letters after your name. Block all distractions, remove all hurdles and invest your time to better understand and prepare yourself completely for this rite of passage. PhD brings with it a feeling of accomplishment, satisfaction and joy that is unmatched and unparalleled to anything else.

The strategies in this book are designed to take you a step closer to achieving your dream. It is my sincere hope that you find the right motivation and encouragement to let go of all inhibitions and choose the path of doctoral degree. I wish you the very best!

Prerequisites for pursuing a PhD

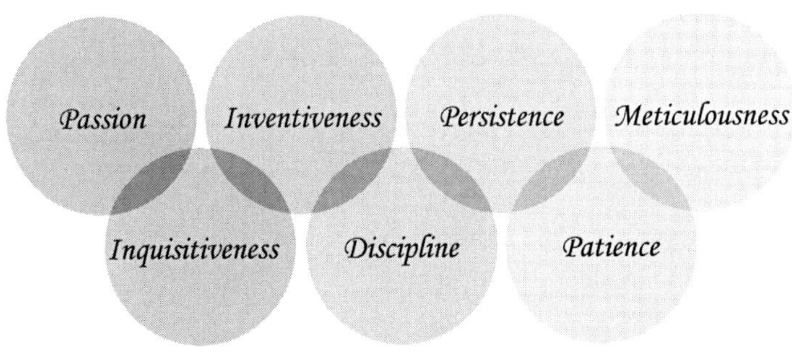

References

- Adhikari, G. R. (2020). Strategies for selecting a research topic. *Mining Engineers' Journal, 22*(1), 27-31.
- Ali, A., & Kohun, F. (2006). Dealing with isolation feelings in IS doctoral programs. *International Journal of Doctoral Studies, 1*, 21-33. http://www.informingscience.us
- Ali, P. A., Watson, R. & Dhingra, K. (2016). Postgraduate research students' and their supervisors' attitudes towards supervision. *International Journal of Doctoral Studies*, *11*, 227–241.
- Ampaw, F. D., & Jaeger, A. J. (2011). Understanding the factors affecting degree completion of doctoral women in the science and engineering fields. *New Directions for Institutional Research, 152*, 59–73.
- Andrade, C. (2011). How to write a good abstract for a scientific paper or conference presentation. *Indian Journal of Psychiatry, 53*(2), 172-175.
- Annesley, T. M. (2010a). Show your cards: The results section and the poker game. *Clinical Chemistry, 56*, 1066-1070.
- Annesley, T. M. (2010a). The discussion section: Your closing argument. *Clinical Chemistry, 56*, 1671-1674.
- Basturkmen, H., East, M. & Bitchener, J. (2014). Supervisors' on-script feedback comments on drafts of dissertations:

Socializing students into the academic discourse community. *Teaching in Higher Education*, *19*, 432–445.

- Bégin, C., & Gérard, L. (2013). The role of supervisors in light of the experience of doctoral students. *Policy Futures in Education*, *11*, 267-276.
- Bitzer, E. M. (2011). Doctoral success as ongoing quality business: A possible conceptual framework. *South African Journal of Higher Education, 25*, 425-443.
- Bocsi, V., Cegledi, T., Kocsis, Z., Kocavs, K. E., Kovacs, K., Muller, A., Pallay, K., Szabo, B. E., Szigeti, F., & Toth, D. A. (2018). The discovery of the possible reasons for delayed graduation and dropout in the light of a qualitative research study. *Journal of Adult Learning Knowledge and Innovation, 2*(2), 27–38. doi:10.1556/2059.02.2018.08
- Brill, J. L., Balcanoff, K. K., Land, D., Gogarty, M., & Turner, F. (2014). Best practices in doctoral retention: Mentoring. *Higher Learning Research Communications, 4*(2), 26-37.
- Castelló, M., Pardo, M., Sala-Bubaré, A., & Suñe-Soler, N. (2017). Why do students consider dropping out of doctoral degrees? Institutional and personal factors. *Higher Education, 74*(6), 1053-1068.
- Cassuto, L. (2013). PhD attrition: How much is too much? Chronicle of Higher Education. https://www.chronicle.com/article/PhD-Attrition-How-Much-Is/140045.
- Council of Graduate Schools (CGS) (2009). PhD completion and attrition: Findings from exit surveys of PhD completers. https://cgsnet.org/phd-completion-and-attrition-findings-exit-surveys-phd-completers-0

- Council of Graduate Schools (CGS) (2012). PhD completion and attrition: Findings from exit surveys of PhD completers. Author.
- Creswell, J. W. (2013). *Qualitative Inquiry and Research Design: Choosing Among Five Approaches* (3rd ed.). Thousand Oaks, CA: Sage Publication.
- Cutler, D., & Lleras-Muney, A. (2010). Understanding differences in health behaviors by education. *Journal of Health Economics, 29*(1), 1-28.
- Derényi, A. (2015). Bizonyítékokra alapozott kormányzás és a kommunikáci´o képzés [An evidence-based training on communication]. *Jelkep*, *4*(1), 1–21. doi:10.20520/Jel-Kep.2015.1.KLSZ.21
- Dawson, C. (2019). Introduction to Research Methods 5th Edition: A Practical Guide for Anyone Undertaking a Research Project. Robinson.160p.
- Devos, C., Boudrenghien, G., Van der Linden, N., Assaad, A., Frenay, M., Galand, B., & Klein, O. (2016). Doctoral students' experiences leading to completion or attrition: A matter of sense, progress and distress. *European Journal of Psychology of Education*. *32*(1), 61-77. https://doi.org/10.1007/s10212-016-0290-0
- Devos, C., Boudrenghien, G., Van der Linden, N., Azzi, A., Frenay, M., Galand, B., & Klein, O. (2017). Doctoral students' experiences leading to completion or attrition: A matter of sense, progress and distress. *European Journal of Psychology of Education, 32*(1), 61-77.
- Dixon, L., Duncan, C., Fagan, J. C., Mandernach, M., & Warlick, S. E. (2010). Finding articles and journals via

Google scholar, journal portals, and link resolvers: Usability study results. Reference & User Services Quarterly, 50(2), 170-181.

- DiscoverPhDs (2019). PhD failure rate – A study of 26,076 PhD candidates. https://www.discoverphds.com/advice/doing/phd-failure-rate
- Erichsen, E. A., Bolliger, D. U., & Halupa, C. (2014). Student satisfaction with graduate supervision in doctoral programs primarily delivered in distance education settings. *Studies in Higher Education*, *39*(2), 321–338. https://doi.org/10.1080/03075079.2012.709496
- Ewing, H., Mathieson, K., Alexander, J. L., & Leafman, J. (2012). Enhancing the acquisition of research skills in online doctoral programs: The Ewing Model. *MERLOT Journal of Online Learning and Teaching, 8*(1): 34-44.
- Ezendam Nicole, P. M., Brug, J., Borsboom, G., van, E. P., & Oenema, A. (2014). Differential effects of the computer-tailored FATaintPHAT programme on dietary behaviors according to sociodemographic, cognitive and home environmental factors. *Public Health Nutrition, 17*(2):431-439.
- Fink, A. (2014). *Conducting Research Literature Reviews: From the Internet to Paper.* Fourth Edition. Thousand Oaks, CA: SAGE.
- Ford, L., & Vaughn, C. (2011). Working together more than alone: Students' evolving perceptions within a four-year educational administration doctoral cohort. *The Qualitative Report, 16*(6), 1645-1668. Retrieved from http://www.nova.edu

- Gardner, S. K. (2010). Contrasting the socialization experiences of doctoral students in high and low-completing departments: A qualitative analysis of disciplinary con-texts at one institution. *The Journal of Higher Education, 81*(1), 61-81.
- Gates, B. (2017). Putting students first. https://www.gatesnotes.com/Education/Georgia-State-University.
- Geraghty, A. W., Torres, L., Leykin, Y., Pérez-Stable, E. J., & Muñoz, R. F. (2013). Understanding attrition from international internet health interventions: A step towards global eHealth. *Health Promotion International, 28*(3), 442-452.
- Ghasemi, A., Bahadoran, Z., Mirmiran, P., Hosseinpanah, F., Shiva, N., & Zadeh-Vakili, A. (2019). The principles of biomedical scientific writing: Discussion. International Journal of Endocrinology and Metabolism, 17(3).
- Grant, C., & Osanloo, A. (2019). Understanding, selecting, and integrating a theoretical framework in dissertation research: Creating the blueprint for your "House." *Administrative Issues Journal, 4*(2), 12-26.
- Gregoric, C., & Wilson, A. (2012). Informal Peer Mentoring During the Doctoral Journey: Perspectives of Two Postgraduate Students. In M. Kiley (Ed.), Proceedings of the 10th Quality in Postgraduate Research Conference: Narratives of Transition: Perspectives of Research Leaders, Educators and Postgraduates (pp. 83-92). Retrieved from http://chelt.anu.edu.au
- Grittner, U., Kuntsche, S., Gmel, G., & Bloomfield, K. (2013). Alcohol consumption and social inequality at the individual and country levels--results from an international study. *European Journal of Public Health, 23*(2), 332-339.

- Groot, W., & Maassen van den Brink M. (2006). What does education do to our health? In: Measuring the Effects of Education on Health and Civic Engagement: Proceedings of the Copenhagen Symposium. 2006 Presented at: Copenhagen Symposium on measuring the effects of education on health and civic engagement; Mar 2006; Copenhagen p. 355-364. http://www.oecd.org/edu/innovation-education/37437718.pdf

- Habibović, M., Cuijpers, P., Alings, M., van der Voort, P., Theuns, D., Bouwels, L., et al. (2014). Attrition and adherence in a WEB-Based Distress Management Program for Implantable Cardioverter defibrillator Patients (WEBCARE): Randomized controlled trial. *Journal of Medical Internet Research, 16*(2), e52.

- Hamid, Z., & Shah, S. A. (2018). Explorations of the interactions between supervisors and their research scholars at University of Kashmir. *International Journal of Education Movement and Social Science, 7*(2), 320-325.

- Henderson, R. (2020). The college dropout rate is 45% - should everyone still go? https://www.google.com/amp/s/www.psychologytoday.com/us/blog/after-service/202006/the-college-dropout-rate-is-45-should-everyone-still-go%3famp

- Herman, C. (2011). Obstacles to success—Doctoral student attrition in South Africa. *Perspectives in Education, 29*(3), 40-52. http://www.perspectives-in-education.com/Default.aspx

- Hiscock, R., Bauld, L., Amos, A., Fidler, J., & Munafò, M. (2012). Socioeconomic status and smoking: A review. *Annals of the New York Academy of Sciences, 1248*(1), 107-123.

- Holley, K., & Caldwell, M. (2012). The challenges of designing and implementing a doctoral student mentoring program. *Innovative Higher Education, 37*, 243-253. http://dx.doi.org/10.1007/s10755-011-0203-y
- Holmes, B. D., Robinson, L., & Seay, A. D. (2010). Getting to finished: Strategies to ensure completion of the doctoral dissertation. *Contemporary Issues in Education Research, 3*(7), 1-8. Retrieved from http://journals.cluteonline.com
- Horta, H., Cattaneo, M., & Meoli, M. (2018). PhD funding as a determinant of PhD and career research performance. *Studies in Higher Education*, *43*(3), 542–570.
- Hulshof, K. F., Brussaard, J., Kruizinga, A., Telman, J., Löwik, M. R. (2003). Socio-economic status, dietary intake and 10 y trends: the Dutch National Food Consumption Survey. *European Journal of Clinical Nutrition, 57*(1), 128-137.
- Iroegbu, E. E., & Agboola, B. M. (2019). Student engagement variables and first year undergraduate retention rate in University of Uyo, Akwa Ibom State, Nigeria. *American Journal of Education and Learning, 4*(1), 98-116.
- Jiranek, V. (2010). Potential predictors of timely completion among dissertation research students at an Australian faculty of sciences. *International Journal of Doctoral Studies, 5,* 1-13. http://ijds.org/Volume5/IJDSv5p001-013Ji-ranek273.pdf
- Jones, M. (2013). Issues in doctoral studies – forty years of journal discussion: Where have we been and where are we going? *International Journal of Doctoral Studies*, *8* (6), 83–104.

- Kim, D., & Otts, C. (2010). The effect of loans on time to doctorate degree: Differences by race/ethnicity, field of study, and institutional characteristics. *Journal of Higher Education, 81*, 1-32. http://dx.doi.org/10.1353/jhe.0.0079
- Korrapati, R. (2016). Five Chapter Model for Research Thesis Writing: 108 Practical Lessons for MS/MBA/M. Tech/M. Phil/LLM/Ph.D Students. Diamond Pocket Books Pvt Ltd.
- Kroemer, T. (2020). Guide to writing results and discussion sections of a scientific article. https://www.goldbio.com/articles/article/Guide-to-results-and-discussion-section.
- Kyvik, S., & Olsen, T. B. (2014). Increasing completion rates in Norwegian doctoral training: Multiple causes for efficiency improvements. *Studies in Higher Education, 39*, 1668-1682. http://dx.doi.org/10.1080/03075079.2013.801427
- Larabee, R. V. (2020). Research guides: Organizing your social sciences research paper: Quantitative methods. https://libguides.usc.edu/writingguide/quantitatative.
- Levecque, K., Anseel, F., De Beuckelaer, A., Van der Heyden, J., & Gisle, L. (2017). Work organization and mental health problems in PhD students. *Research Policy, 46*(4), 868–879. https://doi.org/10.1016/j.respol.2017.02.008
- Lindley, J., Skead, N., & Montalto, M. (2020). Enhancing institutional support to ensure timely PhD completions in law. *Legal Education Review, 30*(1), 1-28.
- Lott, J. L., Gardner, S., & Powers, D. A. (2010). Doctoral student attrition in the STEM fields: An exploratory event history analysis. *Journal of College Student Retention: Research, Theory & Practice, 11*, 247-266. http://dx.doi.org/10.2190/CS.11.2.e

- Martinez, E., Ordu, C., Della Sala, M. R., & McFarlane, A. (2013). Striving to obtain a school-work-life balance: The full-time doctoral student. *International Journal of Doctoral Studies*, *8*, 39-59. http://ijds.org/Volume8/IJDSv8p039-059Martinez0375.pdf

- Mason, M. M. (2012). Motivation, satisfaction, and innate psychological needs. *International Journal of Doctoral Studies*, *7*, 259-277. http://ijds.org/vol-ume7/IJDSv7p259-277Mason0345.pdf

- Mattick, K., Johnston, J., & de la Croix, A. (2018). How to write a good research question. *The Clinical Teacher, 15*(2), 104-108.

- McIntosh, M. (2016). "Publishing Practices in Graduate Supervision in a Canadian Context: A Theoretical and Empirical Analysis of Existing Research," Unpublished report (University of Toronto), 4-7.

- Meeuwisse, M., Severiens, S. E., & Born, M. (2010). Learning environment, interaction, sense of belonging and study success in ethnically diverse student groups. *Research in Higher Education 51*, 528-545.

- Merriam, S. (2009). *Qualitative Research: A Guide to Design and Implementation. Revised and Expanded from Qualitative Research and Case Study Applications in Education*. San Francisco, CA: John Wiley & Sons.

- Murray, E., White, I., Varagunam, M., Godfrey, C., Khadjesari, Z., & McCambridge, J. (2013). Attrition revisited: Adherence and retention in a web-based alcohol trial. *Journal of Medical Internet Research, 15*(8), e162

- Offerman, M. (2011). Profile of the nontraditional doctoral degree student. *New Directions for Adult & Continuing Education, 129*, 21-30. http://dx.doi.org/10.1002/ace.397
- Overall, N. C., Deane, K. L., & Peterson, E. R. (2011). Promoting doctoral students' research self-efficacy: Combining academic guidance with autonomy support. *Higher Education Research & Development*, *30*(6), 791-805.
- Peels, D., Bolman, C., Golsteijn, R. H, de Vries, H., Mudde, A., van Stralen, M. M, et al., (2012). Differences in reach and attrition between Web-based and print-delivered tailored interventions among adults over 50 years of age: Clustered randomized trial. *Journal of Medical Internet Research, 14*(6), e179
- Price, M., Gros, D., McCauley, J., Gros, K., & Ruggiero, K. (2012). Nonuse and dropout attrition for a web-based mental health intervention delivered in a post-disaster context. *Psychiatry*, *75*(3), 267-284.
- Pyhalto, K., Toom, A., Stubb, J., & Lonka, K. (2012). Challenges of becoming a scholar: A study of doctoral students' problems and well-being. *International Scholarly Research Network Education, 2012*, 1-12. http://dx.doi.org/10.5402/2012/934941
- Reinwand, D. A., Crutzen, R., Elfeddali, I., Schneider, F., Schulz, D. N., Smit, E. S, et al., (2015). Impact of educational level on study attrition and evaluation of web-based computer-tailored interventions: Results from seven randomized controlled trials. *Journal of Medical Internet Research, 17*(10), e228.

- Rockinson-Szapkiw, A. J., Spaulding, L. S., Swezey, J., A., & Wicks, C. J. (2014). Poverty and persistence: A model for understanding individuals' pursuit and persistence in a doctor of education program. *International Journal of Doctoral Studies, 9*, 181-190. http://ijds.org/Volume9/IJDSv9p181-203Rockin-son0606.pdf

- Rooij, E., Fokkens-Bruinsma, M., & Jansen, E. (2021). Factors that influence PhD candidates' success: The importance of PhD project characteristics. *Studies in Continuing Education*, 43(1), 48-67.

- Savage, C. (2012). Alcohol and tobacco related health inequity: a population health perspective. *Journal of Addictions Nursing, 23*(1), 72-74.

- Scott, O. T. (2010). An exploratory study of first-semester student attrition in a community college. *Electronic Theses and Dissertations*, Paper 1292. https://doi.org/10.18297/etd/1292

- Snyder, N., Foltz, C., Lendner, M., & Vaccaro, A. R. (2019). How to write an effective results section. *Clinical Spine Surgery, 32*(7), 295-296.

- Spaulding, L. S., & Rockinson-Szapkiw, A. J. (2012). Hearing their voices: Factors doctoral candidates attribute to their persistence. *International Journal of Doctoral Studies*, *7*, 199-219. http://ijds.org/Volume7/IJDSv7p199-219Spaulding334.pdf

- Stallone, M. N. (2011). Factors associated with student attrition and retention in an educational leadership doctoral program. *Journal of College Teaching & Learning 1*(6). http://www.cluteinstitute.com/ojs/index.php/TLC/arti-cle/view/1952/1931

- Stock, W. A. & Siegfried, J. J. (2014). Fifteen years of research on graduate education in economics: what have we learned? *Journal of Economic Education, 45*, 287-303. http://dx.doi.org/10.1080/00220485.2014.942410
- Storms, B. A., Prada, M. J., & Donahue, E. N. (2011). Advising doctoral candidates to degree completion. *Educational Leadership and Administration: Teaching and Program Development, 23*, 85-92. http://files.eric.ed.gov/fulltext/EJ965229.pdf
- Surbhi, S. (2018). Difference Between Research Method and Research Methodology. https://keydifferences.com/difference-between-research-method-and-research-methodology .html
- Terrell, S. R., Snyder, M. M., Dringus, L. P., & Maddrey, E. (2012). A grounded theory of connectivity and persistence in a limited residency doctoral program. *The Qualitative Report, 17*(31), 1-14. http://www.nova.edu/ssss/QR/QR17/terrell.pdf
- Thinkimpact (2021). College dropout rate. https://www.thinkimpact.com/college-dropout-rates/
- Van de Schoot, R., Yerkes, M. A., Mouw, J. M., & Sonneveld, H. (2013). What took them so long? Explaining PhD delays among doctoral candidates. *PLOS One, 8*(7), e68839. http://dx.doi.org/10.1371/journal.pone.0068839
- Vlismas, K., Stavrinos, V., & Panagiotakos, D. (2009). Socio-economic status, dietary habits and health-related outcomes in various parts of the world: A review. *Central European Journal of Public Health, 17*(2), 55-63.
- West, I. J., Gokalp, G., Pena, E. V., Fischer, L., & Gupton, J. (2011). Exploring effective support practices for doctoral

students' degree completion. *College Student Journal, 45*(2), 310-323. http://www.projectinnovation.biz

- Willis, B., & Carmichael, K. D. (2011). The lived experience of late-stage doctoral student attrition in counselor education. *The Qualitative Report, 16*(1), 192-207. http://nsuworks.nova.edu/tqr/vol16/iss1/11

- Wollast, R., Boudrenghien, G., Van der Linden, N., Galand, B., Roland, N., Devos, C., Clercq, M., Klein, O., Azzi, A., & Frenay, M. (2018). Who are the doctoral students who dropout? factors associated with the rate of doctoral degree completion in universities. *International Journal of Higher Education, 7*(4), 143-156.

- Yin, R. K. (2009). *Case Study Research: Design and Methods (4th ed.).* Thousand Oaks, CA: Sage

- Yob, I., & Crawford, L. (2012). Conceptual framework for mentoring doctoral students. *Higher Learning Research Communications, 2*(2), 34-47. http://dx.doi.org/10.18870/hlrc.v2i2.66

- Young, S. N., VanWye, W. R., Schafer, M., Robertson, T. A., & Poore, A. V. (2019). Factors affecting PhD student success. *International Journal of Exercise Science, 12*(1), 34-45.

- Wohlin, C., & Runeson, P. (2021). Guiding the selection of research methodology in industry – academia collaboration in software engineering. Information and Software Technology, 140, 1-14.

Snapshot of Soft Skills!

- Identify your stakeholders and maintain positive relationships with them.
- First impressions are very important.
- Being on time is imperative. This means sticking to the schedule, each time. If you are late, let it be known well in advance.
- Take notes in meetings. You will be surprised what you forget.
- Know your boundaries. Talk with your supervisor about what decisions you should or should not make. Analyze/ review expectations frequently
- Observe and learn from others, yet create your own style. Be careful to not imbibe those traits that are likely to be detrimental.
- Have fun. Make friends. Enjoy what you do.
- Learn from your seniors on how they keep a track of the numerous tasks that they have to accomplish. Having a daily "To do" list helps.
- Before leaving messages on voice mail, write down your message and speak it slowly. For e-mails, learn when to do a "reply all" vs. "reply".
- Make a visible impact in first 100 days of your new role or job
- Understand that it is OK to do mistakes. Ensure that you don't repeat those mistakes.

- Anything that can be measured statistically can be improved. Find a way to implement measurability.
- Criticize in private and praise in public.
- Follow-up and follow-up some more. It will highlight your dedication like nothing else.
- A hand-written thank you note is far better than an e-mail.
- Differentiate yourself from your competition to provide value to your customers. And remember that both competitors and customers can be internal.
- Plan on Monday morning; then assess and take stock on Friday. Track your weekly status without fail.
- Recommend solutions to problems and challenges and identify opportunities.
- Focus on three sides of the triangle – Employees, Customers, and Understanding your company's Business.
- Awareness on priorities will change on daily/monthly basis. Plan proactively.

Dr. Raghu's Guiding Principles

1. Open your mind to new cultures and changes in life. Change is inevitable; the sooner the better.
2. Make friends; get to know people from other states. Take the best of the cultures and understand others point of view. Diversity!
3. Get to know your managers - don't wait: introduce yourself.
4. Read, read, read, not just your text books – Newspapers, listen to radio, subscribe to a journal or newspaper in your areas of interest.
5. Travel- get to know India/USA and most importantly culture and treasures of India/USA. (Insert your own favorite places!)
6. Make good use of time. Enhance your education (MS / MBA / M.Tech / INS / PMP Certifications) or your experience. Live intentionally!
7. Set annual goals to improve yourself. Have a Mission Statement for yourself and Vision for your life.
8. Network, network, and network. Develop and maintain positive relationships with your family, community, co-workers, and managers.
9. Get involved in volunteer activities. Give back to your community and remember where you came from.
10. Leave your foot prints (Employment, Education, and Family).

Driving Forces of Change

- Make a visible impact in first 100 days.
- On time: Work schedule, meetings, & everything.
- Take notes - keep up with documentation.
- Learn the boundaries of the gig.
- Bring your own style.
- Follow-up / Follow-up / Follow-up.
- Have fun - laugh at the ridiculous.
- The feelers are always up for the train coming - before it hits.
- Drive to solution - everything is done in context of solution.

Other Books by Dr. Raghu Korrapati

What is civilization if not a vast and interlinked network of human relationships? With 'The Business of People', Dr Raghu sets out to teach the reader how to make these relationships healthy and mutually beneficial. Dr. Raghu discusses certain characteristics that we all understand but fail to recognise their importance like punctuality, humility, politeness, rationality, prudence, self-supervision, persistence, apologising, assertiveness, taking the initiative, and sense of humour among others.

ISBN-10: 9350832577 ISBN-13: 978-9350832578

Validated management Practices will walk you through the 108 required knowledge and skill areas so that you can develop to balance the 3 critical aspects of management-employees, customers and financials well. While some of the chapters in this book are oriented towards managers working in an Information Technology industry, it will be useful for managers in any industry with practical advice and tips on how to become an effective manager. In addition, the appendices contain extract of mandatory skills for all professionals from Dr Raghu's previous books - '108 pearls of Wisdom' and 'Dr Raghu's Top Ten' - his guiding principles.

ISBN-10: 9351654834 ISBN-13: 978-9351654834

This research applied Bayesian Modeling to medication noncompliance in glaucoma patients. A model-based decision support system using a Bayesian Network was developed to determine whether a patient was complying with the medications prescribed by the physician. The model may be generalized to other business situations where a decision has to be made based on incomplete and uncertain data sets. The purpose of this research was to devise a Bayesian framework to assess the compliance with medication in glaucoma patients.

ISBN-13: 978-0595368396 **ISBN-10: 0595368395**

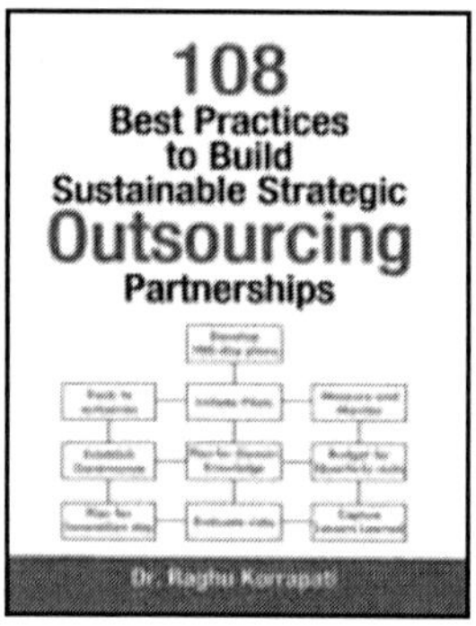

This book is the essence of Dr Korrapati's 30 years of business management experience with highly successful multinational companies, coupled with distilled knowledge of his close interactions with great industry leaders. The book covers - developing a solid outsourcing strategy, deciding what to outsource, negotiating a good deal, keeping the engagement on track, ensuring access to the vendors' best resources, or even terminating a deal in a way that does not harm you. It will benefit everyone, whether you are from a firm that is looking to outsource or a vendor who seeks to establish his company as first choice partner for clients, to gain the advantage you are looking for in the fiercely competitive marketplace.

ASIN: B01JFV7JQM

Leading an organization and its people to success remains a challenge for most managers. With organizations evolving and changing constantly it becomes even more difficult. Management theories and principles often do not provide solutions to the dilemmas that a manager has to deal with in the workplace.

This book by Dr Raghu very adeptly gives some solid answers that managers have sought to be more successful at what they do.

ISBN-10: 8128837575 **ISBN-13: 978-8128837579**

While Dr Raghu Korrapati's 'Passage through India - A tryst with my soul' is an amalgam of Indian experiences of this widely travelled management guru, it is simultaneously also an exposition of his philosophical and spiritual ideas. So, as readers learn numerous lessons in sound management practice presented through Dr Raghu the leader's anecdotes and observations, he/she will be delighted to connect with Dr Raghu the man. Those familiar with Dr Raghu's previous works will be enthralled with another masterpiece on the art and science of management, this time in the context of the master's sojourn as the leader of an India IT organization. 'Passage through India' will, however, will also appeal to those who wish to understand the composer behind the composition, i.e, the mind of a man who successfully runs a large corporate organization.

ISBN-10: 9350836823 **ISBN-13: 978-9350836828**

There is often a considerable gap between the aspirations that many college graduates harbor and the way they go about achieving their goals. While education and technical expertise are often ignore and that defines the difference between an average and a successful career. Dr. Raghu Korrapati has taken it upon himself to identify this 'soft' element and painstakingly elaborated upon its numerous facets. The result is this path-breaking book, which highlights the soft skills that every young graduate and professional needs to possess to reach the pinnacle of professional success. The 108 pearls of wisdom presented here have been drawn from sources as eclectic and diverse as Greek, Indian, Buddhist philosophies, modern day management theory, and psychology. This book has been translated into many languages.

ISBN-10: 8128834223 **ISBN-13: 978-8128834226**

Listed in Best Seller Category

Dr Raghu Korrapati's newest book is a seminal work that is bound to be soon accepted as a significant and powerful contribution to the literature on higher education. This is his landmark effort to encapsulate in one place all that a research scholar might need during his/her research, be it on any subject or discipline. The result is a complex and nuanced picture of the nature, processes, and contexts of research scholarship in varied departmental, disciplinary and institutional cultures.

Undoubtedly, this pivotal and pioneering book will prove to be valuable to both faculty and graduate students who study higher education. Further, institutional leaders, deans, and chairpersons of tenure, and promotion committees who seek to develop vaster comprehension of scholarship will also greatly benefit from this.

Dr Korrapati has mentored thousands of research students in a wide spectrum of disciplines and fields over the span of several decades. This book by him is the latest in a long line of works that have inspired and informed innumerable students and professionals across countries.

ISBN-10: 9352617614 ISBN-13: 9789352617616

A Master Service Agreement (MSA) is a contractual document that specifies performance objectives and outlines the responsibilities of both parties in the agreement. It also lists the current and prospective services to which the agreement applies. MSAs typically state performance objectives as service level agreements – written, measurable processes or service performance targets that the service provider and customer agree on. A statement of work (SOW) is a formal document that captures and defines the work activities, deliverables, and timeline a vendor must execute in performance of specified work for a client. The present study attempted to ascertain the factors in developing MSAs and SOWs and various best practices for alternate dispute resolutions available for offshore software managers. The study adds to the body of knowledge in the areas of Software Intellectual Property Rights, Alignment of MSAs and SOWs, ADR Mechanism for Contractual Breaches, Best Practices in Information Technology, Offshore Management, and Organizational Behavior.

ISBN-10: 1532020686 **ISBN-13: 978-1532020681**

The admission of foreign students to universities and colleges in the United States has two major components: the evaluation of foreign educational credentials, and the administrative process that converts an applicant for admission into an enrolled student. The first component has historically been a source of much ambiguity and trouble to Indian students and professionals vying for places in USA Universities.

Dr Raghu Korrapati, in another glorious attempt at championing the cause of students and young professionals all over India, has come up with this seminal work to eliminate this ambiguity. In this ground-breaking new book, he displays rare acumen, insight, and scholarly prowess to minutely analyse the education systems in the USA and India, before going on to provide painstakingly researched information on each Indian higher education degree and its equivalency with respect to USA degrees. For this reason alone, this book is worth its weight in gold for any Indian student planning to study in the USA or an Indian professional aiming to work in the USA.

Apart from the students, there are numerous other institutions and individuals who will benefit from the wonderful content present in the book – USA admission officers and universities, USA employers hiring Indians on H1B visas, licensors, USA state/federal agencies, and immigration attorneys. The amount of detail on the USA education system that has been offered by the matchless Dr Korrapati will also help Indian educational administrators.

ISBN-10: 9352619870 **ISBN-13: 978-93-5261-987-0**

H-1B visas play a very important role in hiring foreign born skilled workers for Specialty Occupations in the United States. This visa system has largely benefited the U.S economy, benefitting the I.T industry the most, with the flow of skilled foreign-born employees. Due to the growing concerns over misuse and a perceived threat to domestic jobs, stricter scrutiny on H-1B petitions has increased in the past few years.

This book aims at demystifying the myths surrounding "Specialty Occupations" not only to the employers, but also to petitioners, academics, attorneys, students and other interested parties. It also aims at filling the gap in the research and understanding on Specialty Occupations. There is no comprehensive text or authority on this important issue and all the information available is only through the policy memoranda of USCIS, judgments in appealed petitioners and blogs of attorneys.

This book tries to provide a better understanding of the issue and also identifies some common errors in H-1B petitions and aims to be a one-stop reference to employers, attorneys and expert opinion evaluators on the issue

ISBN-10: -- 9352787708 ISBN-13: 978-93-5278-770-8

This book is updated version of previous years book. Based on receiving huge compliments from prior version, this book includes updates for years 2019-20. Several new guidelines in the area of Minimum Requirements for proffered position, Interview requirements for Specialty occupations questionnaire, sample job description templates, Guidelines on generic "Engineering" or "Business Administration" degrees, and new requirements for evaluators.

This book aims at demystifying the myths surrounding "Specialty Occupations" not only to the employers, but also to petitioners, academics, attorneys, students and other interested parties. It also aims at filling the gap in the research and understanding on Specialty Occupations. There is no comprehensive text or authority on this important issue and all the information available is only through the policy memoranda of USCIS, judgments in appealed petitioners and blogs of attorneys.

This book tries to provide a better understanding of the issue and also identifies some common errors in H-1B petitions and aims to be a one-stop reference to employers, attorneys and expert opinion evaluators on the issue.

ISBN-10: 9352969227 **ISBN-13: 978-93-5296-922-7**

There is tremendous ambiguity surrounding this field. It is compounded by the fact that grading systems differ widely in theory and practice from one country to another, and the fair interpretation of foreign grades into national ones is a major concern, both for students returning after a study period abroad and for university staff required to assess the credentials of foreign applicants. The academic world, especially students, struggle to determine what their education amounts to in another country.

The credential evaluation component also exists outside of the academic community: at state licensing boards and other types of governmental agencies, at professional associations, and at private foreign educational credential evaluation services which assist institutions and agencies that do not have in-house expertise. This book is also aimed to facilitate the smoother functioning of these institutions.

ISBN-10: 9352969219 ISBN-13: 978-93-5296-921-0

It is often said that salespeople would rather sell than spend a day learning how to do it. They think time is money and every hour spent in training is money lost and time wasted. But what they fail to understand is that learning how to do sales effectively is actually a catalyst for great sales results for the organization and excellent sales performance for the individual. It is worth noting that while sales is one of the easiest careers to get into, it is not as easy to sustain and spend a life in. So to put it in simpler words, ***"Everyone can be a sales person, but not everyone can be a successful sales person".*** To be a successful salesperson it is important to have a deep understanding of the industry you cater to. While the general skill set remains the same, it is the deeper and niche understanding that has the power to differentiate the best from the rest.

In the market, there are numerous books and articles on various sales techniques available. In this book, I am discussing the 'Nine habits of highly effective software sales professionals'. The title gives you a broad idea of what this book is all about, but more than nine habits, it is packed with 30 years of my personal and professional experience in the software industry and managing clients. I provided more emphasis on how successful sales professionals, sales leaders and their companies organize themselves with short-term and long-term planning and adopt disciplined execution on those plans.

ISBN-10: 9352969200　　ISBN-13: 978-93-5296-920-3

"Academic Publishing" by Dr Raghu Korrapati is a comprehensive guide to provide deep insights into academic publishing and how to avoid costly pitfalls. Being a scholar practitioner and publisher himself with over three decades years of academic and executive leadership work experience, Dr Korrapati has distilled key facets of academic publishing into nine core chapters ranging from the step-by-step process of academic publication to measuring the impact of published work while focusing on publication ethics and avoiding misconduct. Each chapter provides guiding principles and builds the foundation toward guiding you to become a successful scholar-publisher. Use this book as a guide to help you navigate the path toward becoming a great scholar publisher.

ISBN-10: 9355990405 **ISBN-13: 978-93-5599-040-2**

Notes

Notes

Notes

Notes